The
Little Book
of Moods

101 Ways to Identify and Deal with Any Emotion!

Jane Eldershaw

Adams Media
Avon, Massachusetts

Published by
Adams Media, an F+W Publications Company
57 Littlefield Street, Avon, MA 02322 U.S.A.
www.adamsmedia.com

ISBN: 1-59337-060-1

Printed in Canada.

J I H G F E D C B A

Library of Congress Cataloging-in-Publication Data
Eldershaw, Jane.
The little book of moods / Jane Eldershaw.
p.   cm.
ISBN 1-59337-060-1
1. Conduct of life. 2. Mood (Psychology) I. Title.
BF637.C5E383 2004
152.4—dc22
2003023154

This publication is designed to provide accurate and authoritative information with regard to the subject matter covered. It is sold with the understanding that the publisher is not engaged in rendering legal, accounting, or other professional advice. If legal advice or other expert assistance is required, the services of a competent professional person should be sought.

—From a *Declaration of Principles* jointly adopted by a Committee of the
American Bar Association and a Committee of Publishers and Associations

Many of the designations used by manufacturers and sellers to distinguish their products are claimed as trademarks. Where those designations appear in this book and Adams Media was aware of a trademark claim, the designations have been printed in initial capital letters.

Cover illustration by Jan Bryan Hunt.

This book is available at quantity discounts for bulk purchases.
For information, call 1-800-872-5627.

Contents

1. impoverished
feel like a millionaire

● What's your definition of luxury? Wearing real cashmere? A huge plate of fresh oysters all for yourself? A spritz of Joy perfume every morning? Going first class when you usually fly steerage? A split of champagne with lunch? Luxury isn't so much in the thing itself, it's in the details: Having an *overabundance* of raspberries, taking a taxi when you usually walk, having a hot shower after a week of camping. To feel rich, know what your luxuries are and get a little on a regular basis— but not too much, too often, because then they won't be luxuries anymore.

"There are people who have money and people who are rich."
—Coco Gabrielle Chanel

We must attend to our own well-being. In fact, we are the only ones who can do it properly.

Taking better care of your money is the same thing as taking better care of yourself.

Money *does* buy happiness, but once the basics have been satisfied, it's our attitude toward money that's more important than how much we have. Act like a poor person and that's what you are.

● Spoil yourself with little treats: Take the afternoon off; try a new toothpaste; splurge on $15 worth of caviar; buy yourself a present and have it gift-wrapped; get a subscription to *Oprah* magazine; have your nails done; test-drive a BMW.

● Choose your favorite painting at a local museum. Picasso? Matisse? You can visit it every day and get to know its every nuance. You will "own" that Picasso in a much more authentic way than the billionaire who barely glances at *his* Picasso.

inner affluence

Try choosing the absolute best—not necessarily the most expensive—option in all the little things for a feeling of inner affluence. Do this to generate that feeling of well-being that being good to yourself brings—and because you deserve the best!

▶ Order the meal you really want at a restaurant instead of the least expensive one.
▶ Use a real sponge.
▶ Use a beautiful pair of chopsticks.
▶ Use a gorgeous spectacle case.

It's not so much greedy as symbolically life-affirming.

Use the good china every day.

"You don't have to be rich, you just have to learn to live rich."
—Beverly Pepper

be like a wealthy socialite: Help a worthy cause. Give your time rather than money and discover how prosperous you really are.

2.IRRITABLE

the soothing power of words

Keep a folder of favorite quotes, but add anything that uplifts you and makes you feel good; anything that speaks to you in some way. If you are a visual person, it might be a picture, a reproduction of a painting, a photograph, or even an advertisement torn from a magazine. Sift through the collection to meet the need of the mood you are in or to find inspiration, comfort, or laughter.

Appreciate words of wisdom wherever you find them—scraps of movie dialogue, graffiti, stories, cartoons. Language is how we shape our thoughts, and a different way of stating an idea can give you new insight and clarify your thinking. Repeating the words of a soul-shuddering quote reinforces the spiritual lesson.

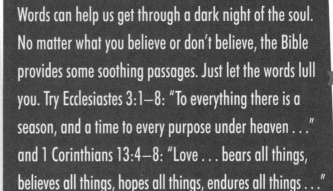

Words can help us get through a dark night of the soul. No matter what you believe or don't believe, the Bible provides some soothing passages. Just let the words lull you. Try Ecclesiastes 3:1–8: "To everything there is a season, and a time to every purpose under heaven . . ." and 1 Corinthians 13:4–8: "Love . . . bears all things, believes all things, hopes all things, endures all things . . ."

Carl Jung, one of the founders of psychoanalysis, believed that everyone, all over the world, shares a common evolutionary history, so we interpret experiences—things like birth, death, the sun, mothers, fathers, heroes, demons, wise men—in a similar way. He called them archetypes. They're common to all societies and form the basis of myths and folk stories that people have told and drawn sustenance from through the ages.

Children's books can be comforting. Before you go to sleep, re-read one that you loved as a child (or discover one you've never read) to take your mind off adult troubles. Try some classics: *The Wind in the Willows* by Kenneth Grahame or *Charlotte's Web* by E. B. White or *Alice in Wonderland* by Lewis Carroll.

Poetry-phobic? School can sometimes do that to you. But out of all the kinds of verse ever composed, there must be *some* that make you happy. Try a book of popular selections from the past. Read a poem aloud—its rhythm will be calming. The words of the famous poets of the past evoke powerful images, like this:

There is sweet music here that softer falls
Than petals from blown roses on the grass . . .
Music that gentlier on the spirit lies,
Than tired eyelids upon tired eyes . . .
—*Alfred Lord Tennyson, "Song of the Lotus-Eaters"*

Having a Pollyanna attitude may not solve your problems, but it annoys the hell out of other people—reason enough to try it!

Optimistic people reframe naturally, by looking at a situation from a different point of view, and therefore changing the way they respond to it. Try it yourself. Instead of dreading your job, re-cast your obnoxious colleagues as characters in a TV sitcom, and you may find yourself coming up with an idea for a screenplay. You'll become eager to get to work to write down more dialogue.

Are you good at the type of pencil-and-paper puzzles in which a single line solves a mathematical equation or connects all the dots? The line turns out to be one that transforms a plus sign into the numeral 4, or one that extends beyond what you thought were the boundaries of the puzzle. The answer requires a shift in your perspective to see the solution. These types of puzzles are good practice for turning your thinking around.

Our greatest weaknesses are always the flip side of our greatest strengths.

"Start every day off with a smile and get it over with."
—W. C. Fields

3. Optimistic
looking on the bright side

Reframing is the technique that made fictional character Pollyanna famous, and her name has come to represent an annoying, goody-two-shoes attitude. That's because other people usually try to reframe for you—when one has an outsider's perspective, it's easy to see the answers to another's problems. Friends are reframing when they tell you, for example, that you're lucky to live in a walk-up because it means you don't need to go to a gym to use the Stairmaster; or that getting fired was a blessing because you hated the job.

There are two types of reframing: *context* reframing and *content* reframing. Context reframing occurs when you realize that something seemingly undesirable is actually desirable in another context (manure turns into fertilizer when you put it on a garden!). Content reframing occurs when you decide to change your interpretation of a situation so you have more positive thoughts about it. (You're waiting in line? Instead of considering it a waste of time, enjoy the ten-minute time-out to do a crossword puzzle, chat with the people in line with you, or read the trashy magazines.)

> Any time you want to sell something, find its selling points by reframing. Remember, it's not a bug, it's a feature.

4. disorganized

the meaning behind clutter

Organize your life by making it more colorful! You'll find the rush jobs in a file drawer quickly if they are all in bright yellow hanging files. Color also helps you to identify different departments or types of memos (urgent on blue paper, news on pink) and to organize by time periods or subjects.

When you've clarified your personal goals, you'll know what you are clearing a path toward. Replace a vague desire to tidy up with the aim of getting rid of the things that don't contribute to your goal.

• Having excess junk is like hauling a suitcase around: It's a nuisance and restricts you.

• If you never look at that abandoned craft project, you're not working on it— and if you feel guilty about it, it's draining you of energy rather than helping you. Toss it out.

Don't agonize, organize!

Buy organizing systems that you love the look of and that make sense to you; otherwise, you won't use them.

• Feel at home in a mess? Maybe you're a creative person who's afraid of throwing out inspiration, or a perfectionist who finds it difficult to make decisions. Possessions come to mean opportunities or emotional security to us; that may be why you can't bear to part with a single thing. If you discover the deeper psychological issues behind your disorder, you can be more effective in dealing with it.

Feeling comfortable at home means feeling comfortable with yourself.

A mess is a tangle of postponed decisions.

Determine the real way you use something, the real way it serves you. If what you want from your photos is to be able to find the pictures of the trips to Paris when you need them, don't stick them in photo albums organized by year, put them in boxes sorted by person or event.

When putting something away, ask yourself: Where would I look for this if it were lost? When you are tidying up, interrogate each item:

What is your function in my life?

Where do you belong?

Point-of-use storage is the most practical: If all your makeup ends up in the bathroom, put extra shelves there to hold it, rather than carting it back to the bedroom every day.

• *Being organized doesn't necessarily mean being neat and tidy. If living surrounded by clutter doesn't distract you, if you can find what you want when you want it, you are organized.*

5. easygoing
feel this way more often

Take a pleasure break. Every day.

Have fun. It's better than Botox.

Mental health, like physical health, depends on being in balance, with each component part working harmoniously together. Our moods are like the tides, ever-shifting. To stay balanced, be aware of your thoughts and what you tell yourself about what's happening.

*B*e someone who loves life. Be someone who gets excited about little things, things like the first signs of spring or baby ducklings or a new book by your favorite author. People will smile at you patronizingly—it's so easy to make you happy. But isn't that better than being the reverse, someone who is easily made unhappy?

Don't let anyone else tell you what you ought to consider fun. If it gets boring fast, you regret it later, or it makes someone else unhappy, don't do it—even if it's what most people your age do.

$\mathcal{W}$hat did happiness mean in your family when you were growing up? That definition doesn't have to be your definition now that you are an adult. Especially question a belief that relies on someone else or something else to provide happiness.

The way you choose to see the world creates the world you see.

You can decide to be miserable or you can decide to be happy. Try it and see.

$\mathcal{L}$ike anything you spend time caring for, your happy moods will grow if you nurture and appreciate them. Start by thinking about how you sabotage yourself, what you do that prevents your being happy. At the end of your life you want to be able to say that you loved every minute of it.

"Love can't buy happiness, marriage can't buy happiness, only happiness can buy happiness."
—Merle Shain

It's not what happens to us in life that determines our happiness, but the way we react to what happens.

Maybe it's time to try something new. If your only ways of having fun are movies or the mall, it's definitely time to widen your options.

$\mathcal{A}$ lot of feelings of unhappiness—joylessness, frustration, hopelessness—disappear when you are doing work that is the essence of you, that you were meant to do, that feels right.

▶ **How does one meditate?** Sit comfortably (you don't have to be in the lotus position). Close your eyes. Focus your whole awareness on your breathing. Feel each breath as it enters and leaves your body. Do this for a few minutes. ❧ Then visualize a lighted candle. See any random thought as a breeze that makes the flame waver—aim to keep it straight. Your thoughts will start drifting, that's what thoughts do. Don't dwell on them or push them out of your mind, just notice them, as if they were the flickering images on a TV set in a shop window. Don't get caught up in them. ❧ Ideally you'd do this for about twenty minutes, then stretch and slowly "re-enter" the world.

There's no way of forcing tension out of yourself—you must let it float away.

▶ **The easy way to meditate:** Go for a walk. Walking meditation is easy. The repetitive, rhythmic motion soothes your body, and your mind seems more in touch with subconscious thoughts. You don't have to change the way you walk, just be aware of your body and the physical sensations it feels. Focus on your breathing, your footsteps, or on something in the landscape, and let everything else fall away. Try to balance equally your awareness of what your body is feeling and what you notice of the outer world. Or you can repeat a phrase or poem to yourself in sync with your steps.

6. restless

tranquility through meditation

▶ **Why meditate?** Because it's the best way to cope with stress, and because it will gradually lead to a quiet, centered, relaxed, nonjudgmental state of mind. When you can brush aside distracting thoughts, negative emotions that you usually avoid may surface, but you'll be able to examine them impartially and become more aware of the real, inner you.

Just shutting your eyes **quiets** a lot of activity in your brain and may be enough to **calm** you down in the middle of a busy day when you can't meditate.

It takes time to appreciate the calming benefits of meditation. It has a cumulative effect—give it time to work. Commit yourself to meditating regularly for a period of time before you decide it isn't for you.

If you are in surroundings where you are bombarded with stimuli, instead of trying to fight off the sound and action, let them wash through you. *Retreat into interior stillness.*

7. threatened

pacifying anger

Anger isn't always violent: Sarcasm, incredulity, caustic humor, put-downs, and malicious gossiping are forms of anger. Passive aggression is indirectly expressed anger—that's when someone is unhelpful or hostile when asked to do things, or when he deliberately misunderstands instructions or spreads rumors and creates discord to sabotage whatever he's involved in.

Humor can sometimes defuse hostility. Gently point out the ridiculous side of the situation.

Anger is one of the basic emotions humans developed to protect themselves. It's a response to fear, frustration, loss, and disappointment; it's the protective side of hurt.

Adopt a calm, accepting approach with someone who is aggressive—it's only emotional energy that needs to be vented. Let the angry person know that her feelings are recognized, by saying "I can see you are upset" or "I understand that you're feeling angry," and encourage displacement activities, such as physical exercise—talk it over as you go for a walk. Ask for clarification and amplification, not justification.

When someone is hostile and angry, you have three choices: You can let her pull you into her emotional turmoil and respond with your own anger; you can let her anger overwhelm you and react emotionally (by crying, for example); or you can try to step outside yourself, be aware of your own reactions, and control them. The best thing to do is to pull back from an argument and look at it as objectively as possible.

How did your parents handle anger? Are you reliving old scenarios? Perhaps you are unable to show your own anger but provoke someone close to you into showing aggression.

You can't force someone who often makes you angry to change his ways. In real life, crabby people rarely do a quick metamorphosis into lovable people even when treated nicely. The only person you can control is yourself—the only reactions you can influence are your own.

Levels of testosterone seem to influence a person's tendency toward violence, delinquency, suicide, heroic altruism, and aggression. But as with most hormones, the level of testosterone in the blood can go up and down depending on stress levels. Testosterone affects behavior, but the outcome of behavior also affects testosterone levels—fans at a soccer match can experience higher testosterone levels if their team wins.

8. MISMATCHED

You should complete your own homework before you join your life with someone else's. Can you recognize both the good and bad in your parents and identify those same qualities in yourself? Who in your family does the person you love resemble? How does that make you feel? And is that good or bad? What kind of person does he need you to be, and is that who you really are? Think about the type of people you've been attracted to in the past. Which of you was more in love? Who was more in control?

Looking for the perfect "other" who will make you feel successful, beautiful, and worthwhile? Big mistake. So is marrying so you won't feel lonely or feeling that you can only enjoy life with someone else—the marriage will have to carry the whole burden of your existence. And if you think the bad relationship you are in is better than none, ask yourself what you fear. Where did that lack of confidence come from?

Do you communicate well, stimulate each other mentally, have a similar sense of humor, and a shared vision for how you want to live your life?

Why do people stay in relationships that are clearly so wrong? Often they feel compelled to keep trying to gain the love and attention of someone—their mother or father—who wasn't able to give it to them when they were a child. For example, someone who keeps choosing an unresponsive partner and hopes to change him is probably still trying to make unresponsive parents care.

Needing someone desperately is not love. The more whole you are as a person, the less you'll need to control someone else, the less you'll strive to get others to give you what you want.

Hold your spouse responsible for how he treats you, not for how you feel about yourself. Don't cast him as your conscience ("Don't let me eat too much!") or give him a role as a father figure.

Only people with a solid sense of self are mature enough to merge their life with someone else and not fear losing themselves.

If you're looking for a lover, search for a friend.

Never commit to a person you don't trust and can't respect.

What matters most is not so much how he feels about you, but how he feels about himself.

Have you ever noticed yourself picking up the tempo of the people around you? Make a *conscious effort* not to react to jerky traffic movement, staccato media noise, or rushing commuters. *Plug into* slow music, or spend half an hour in an environment where people move slowly, such as a park, a flower shop, or a church. *Unwind into* the more leisurely rhythm.

Try to expel every bit of old air from your lungs and the next breath will automatically be deep and energy-giving.

9. Excitable

breathe in calm

Oxygen is the gas your body runs on. Any time you need more energy, take a deep breath to send more oxygen—fuel—to your muscles.

eel the calming effects of deep breathing for yourself: Take a few quick little shallow gasps—instant stress. Your body starts reacting as if danger were imminent, and you begin to feel anxious. Now breathe deeply and slowly—immediate relaxation. Your heartbeat and brain waves slow; you're calmer. Whenever you feel overexcited, you can calm yourself by taking a deep breath.

Normal breathing is about twelve to fourteen breaths a minute. Try to slow it down to eight deep breaths a minute.

Don't be afraid that you are deep breathing the "wrong" way. You don't need to know special yoga techniques—in fact, trying to breathe in a certain way can be stressful! Just breathe so that your tummy goes in and out like a balloon as you inhale and exhale.

The part of our brain that registers smells is the same part that governs the emotions and memories, so the feelings that are aroused by fragrance are strong and direct. One of the easiest and quickest ways to change your mood is with an odor that evokes pleasant memories. Experiment to find a scent that calms you. Try *lavender:* If it soothes, buy a perfume spray to keep with you as your own personal smelling salts. Or keep *vanilla* in your kitchen for both cooking and calming. *Chamomile* is a feel-good scent, too. Brew some chamomile tea and see if the calming effect works for you. Sniff *lemon, jasmine,* and *peppermint* during the sleepy midafternoon hours for alertness.

Swell smells: a fire in the fireplace, fresh-cut grass, crayons, onions frying, sea spray, bread baking, good coffee.

As you breathe, make up your own soothing mantra: "Breathe in calm, breathe out sadness, breathe in joy, breathe out hassles, breathe in energy, breathe out anxiety, breathe in happiness..."

The psychologically healthy person is fully integrated. His spontaneous, unrestrained impulses are not at war with the "parent" side of him: his self-control, his sense of responsibility, his conscience.

Don't be reckless with other people's hearts, other people's money, or other people's lives.

Know what risks you can safely take, avoid hit-or-miss impulsivity, and aim for good timing and good judgment. As with cooking, it takes practice to know when you can depart from the recipe. Before adding more flavoring to a cake, you have to know whether you'll just get a more intensely flavored cake or create a disastrous chemical reaction.

Is the restlessness of taking risks a desire to give birth to a new you? To feel more alive? Or are you trying to get rid of pain and disturbing thoughts? Survivors of abuse often resort to self-destructive behaviors in their struggle to gain a sense of control over their psychological pain. People suffering from bipolar disorder go through intensely manic, impulsive moods. Risk-taking behavior may be a symptom of an illness that can be treated.

10. IMPULSIVE

taking risks safely

Take a pen and piece of paper and draw a line (like a graph from a heart monitor) representing how you would like life to be—would it show regular peaks of excitement every so often? Or gentle ups and downs but no sharp, jagged highs or lows? Sketch a line that indicates just how much stimuli you'd like and how often. Next, draw a line representing how your life actually is. If there's a big difference, you need to make changes.

Risk looking ridiculous: Tell the hairdresser to chop it all off. Crash a party. Make a fool of yourself for love.

What's a risk for some people—traveling to a foreign country alone, writing to a favorite author, calling up a company they want to work for—is unexceptional for others. Limiting beliefs can keep you from taking any risks, fear of facing up to your real needs can cause you to distract yourself by taking unnecessary risks.

We tend to get into a groove as we get older. Comfortable, but boring. Take a risk to feel a little more alive, to test the boundaries of your being.

If you do things to get a thrill from behavior that you know is physically dangerous, talk with a therapist to recognize the fear that leads you to flirt with death.

Risk being yourself.

11. envious

the wish behind the want

There's a reason runners never look back. If you concentrate on someone else's performance, your own suffers.

Is fire a "better" element than air? Are plants "better" than animals? In nature, everything just is.

Do you catch yourself putting someone down, belittling another's achievement, or patronizing another's accomplishment? That's envy—but don't try to suppress it. The things you envy most in other people are the things you want most for yourself. They indicate what's really important to you. Transform the pain of jealousy into energy to get for yourself what you need. ✍ What does your yearning represent? Look for themes, not specifics. ✍ What does another's accomplishment symbolize? You may not actually want the identical job your friend has, but you do want the same sort of success in your career. ✍ Make use of an envious mood to set goals for yourself. If you are sure something that someone else has—a law degree, real estate, a husband—will improve your life, start planning to acquire it for yourself.

"The less satisfaction we derive from being ourselves,

● **In some families, children gauge their worth by the amount of attention they receive compared with their siblings, and they feel compelled to prove themselves by comparison and competition.** Your feelings of envy were probably justified back then, but now they don't do you any good. You need to come to terms with the coping mechanisms you developed to deal with being ignored. Instead of seeking out proof that others have more of everything than you do, acknowledge the pain and concentrate on building your sense of self-worth.

Sometimes you're ahead of everyone else; sometimes you're behind. A life spent concentrating on getting and having and comparing is a long, lonely battle. Keep score with others and you'll forever feel smaller and worse off.

Once you can see people for who they are, instead of how they compare to you, and things for what they are, rather than how they can serve you, life is much more relaxed.

● Let someone else grab the only cab, or squeeze in before you at the supermarket, or have the last slice of cake. Why bother to compete with others on this level? Give yourself treats, so your inner child knows there's lots to go around.

the greater is our desire to be like others."—Eric Hoffer

To travel more pleasantly, follow these tips:

* **Alleviate jet lag by increasing blood flow to your head.** Lie on your back on the floor, with legs propped against the wall at a right angle to your body, for a few minutes.

* **Making a list of everything you take makes re-packing easier and is useful if you need to file an insurance claim.** When you get home, update the list with things you wish you'd taken, and keep it for next time.

* **Check everything.** Watch that your luggage gets a tag with the correct three-letter destination code, and that the cases are actually placed on the conveyer belt.

* **To eat good, cheap, authentic food in a place that's new to you, avoid the tourist traps**—find an ethnic neighborhood, university campus, or working people's hangout. Or ask a butcher, a grocer, or baker which local restaurant he eats at himself.

* **To be happy in the air, pick the right seats on the plane:** For a good view, sit away from the wings. For more legroom, sit next to an emergency exit or just behind the bulkhead. With small children, sit near the toilets for easy access. If you want to sleep, sit away from the galley.

> Travel at home: Read the Russians, from Dostoevsky to Chekov; rent *Dr. Zhivago*; drink vodka.

> *"The most precious gift to bring back from a journey is the ability to see the extraordinary in the everyday."*
> —Eric Hansen

12. adventurous

what are you escaping?

"An expatriate travels not to find a new home but a new self."

—E. B. White

*P*lanning to take off with a backpack to "find yourself" or move to another state for the "quality of life"? You really don't have to go anywhere to find either. The things you want to escape from, like the things you want to run to, are within you. *

Of course, one can gain insight from new surroundings and reconnect with what's important by ditching a comfortable routine. The crucial thing is whether the impulse to flee is self-destructive, and whether you're subconsciously trying to avoid facing up to yourself or to getting old.

"... if a fish came to me and said he was going on a journey, I should say, 'With what porpoise?'"

"Don't you mean 'purpose'?" said Alice.
—Lewis Carroll
(*Alice in Wonderland*)

A journey is more interesting when you go with a porpoise—or a purpose. When you read up on the ruins, or learn how to make authentic paella, or record it all in your sketchbook—you're no longer a tourist.

13. VAIN VAIN VAIN

There are people who walk into a room and say, "Here I am, folks!" and people who walk in and say, "Ahhh! There you are!"

A certain amount of vanity about our appearance is normal; it means we take care of our bodies. And a healthy person asks for respect, and appreciates praise. But a narcissist thinks his identity is his image, and is constantly looking to others to provide a mirror, needing them to reflect back unremitting admiration. This is an addiction, a need that has to be filled over and over.

In classical mythology, Narcissus was a handsome young man who became so infatuated with his own reflection in a pond he rejected everything and everyone else. If you are someone who cares about your appearance, others might call you a narcissist, but to psychiatrists, the word is the name of a personality disorder that makes those who have it very difficult to live with. A narcissist is hypersensitive to criticism and reacts with rage, humiliation, or shame to any suggestion that he is less than perfect. He feels more entitled to prestige than other people and always expects unreasonably special treatment. He tends to exaggerate his talent and to aggrandize his ancestors or where he comes from; he lacks feeling for anyone else and is usually egotistical and selfish. It's a painful affliction.

Wanting fame is wanting a mirror held up to you so you can see yourself in it and be reassured that you exist.

Beware of becoming involved with a narcissist, a person with the self-absorption and demands of a two-year-old. Because of how he was treated as a child, the narcissist believes, deep down, that he is nothing, so he needs others to confirm he exists. The less he likes himself, the more he has to convince people how wonderful he is. Narcissists tend to be good at starting relationships but need much stroking and reassurance. They lead their lives defensively, constantly alert to attack, exhausting themselves in the effort.

A healthy person listens to herself, to what she really wants and needs, as a good parent would, rather than to the reactions and applause of other people. A healthy person is convinced of her own worth and finds adoration suffocating.

A narcissist does not love, she lets herself be loved.

14.

Uncoordinated

feel alive
through
your body

Overcome your distaste for the gym by finding a form of full-body movement that allows physical release and creative expression. Dancing lets you express your natural grace. Losing yourself in the movement and surrendering your body to the rhythm of the music can give you a totally absorbing, natural high.

Don't let any past criticism of your musical abilities interfere with your ability to have fun making your own music now. ♪ You can sing to yourself or out loud; you can sing what's on your mind to a familiar tune, or sing positive statements to an advertising jingle. ♪ You can use your voice to energize yourself or to relax. ♪ You can hum a favorite melody in the bath or sing along with the radio while driving. ♪ Belt it out! Sing until you are hoarse and jubilant and elated. ♪ Don't let your happiness be held hostage by anyone else's idea of what sounds good. Have fun with your voice.

Moving in rhythm is one of the most basic urges our bodies have. Don't be constricted by feeling there's a way you "ought" to dance; just put on music and give in to the urge to move. Dancing could be defined as loving yourself and letting your body show it.

All stretching is invigorating because it loosens muscles that are tight and contracted, and increases the blood supply to them. Take a yoga class or learn just one stretch from a book for times you need to calm down. Find one that eases the place where tension accumulates in your body: your neck and shoulders, lower back, or feet.

Music can act as a mood-altering drug:

It's not the lyrics that soothe; it's the rhythm. ♪ Therapists call it the isomodic principle: the fact that different kinds of music have different effects on your mood. ♪ Use this idea to feel better: First, play music that matches your existing mood; then gradually change to songs that have good associations for you until the tempo reflects the kind of mood you'd like to be in. ♪ Go from music with percussion, accented beats, and rhythm, for example, to something with a slow tempo like classical music with string instruments or woodwinds. ♪ Music that is slower than your pulse is more likely to relax you.

Music can be soothing and energizing at the same time—
the pulsating beat is energizing
and moving your body to the beat is soothing.

15. ANGRY

QUENCHING RAGE

● Know that you have a choice about how to react to angry thoughts. The key to controlling yourself is to find a different way of reacting.

The right way of dealing with anger: Aim to express it nonviolently, at the time it arises, at the appropriate person. Resolve to use the energy anger generates to achieve worthwhile goals. The wrong way: displacing anger, trying to bury it, expressing it too late, or using it as an excuse for destructive behavior.

● When you feel yourself getting angry, ask yourself if it's worth it. Try to turn your thoughts to problem-solving mode. Instead of thinking how you can get back at a person, think how you can change the situation.

An assertiveness course will help you express your anger in more effective, positive ways.

● **The longer you keep having angry thoughts about an incident, the angrier you'll get. Your body will start pumping adrenaline into the bloodstream, your heart will beat faster, your blood pressure and blood cholesterol levels will rise, and your immune system will go on hold . . . don't do this to yourself.**

One particular person always provokes hostile feelings? Decide, in advance, how you can deal with him and modify your response. ✍ Your sister-in-law always makes catty comments? ✍ In your mind, step back and become an observer—rate her performance, compare her to Joan Rivers, see the humor in it ✍ She can't hurt you if you won't be hurt.

ANGER FIRST AID: If you feel out of control, go somewhere where you can be alone. Even if your anger is entirely justified, you'll be more effective in retaliation if you have control over yourself. When you are calm, try to work out the real reason you're angry. Diagnose the threat to your well-being. What is the injustice or unmet need here? What do I need to do to let go of this feeling? What is the message I'm getting from this situation?

● Surprised by your own unexpected, intense, vicious, angry reaction to a situation? Your unconscious is telling you that this is something you should deal with, a long-ago hurt that hasn't been resolved. This is where therapy can help. The angry reaction is hiding something that you have to face up to. Painful though it may be, you need to prod the place in your psyche that is bruised; you need to find the real issue behind your anger.

Yawn. Do the action, even if it is an artificial yawn. Stretching the mouth reduces the tension in your jaw, so soon you will really yawn and feel tired.

• When you're sleep-deprived, your good mood is the first thing to go. (Along with creativity, energy, memory, concentration, and coordination. Your stress hormone levels go up and you lose the power of sleep to fight off sickness, too.) When people are deprived of sleep they quickly show signs of mental disturbance. Lack of sleep can be both a cause and an effect of emotional problems. You could probably improve the quality of your life by sleeping more.

• Try a sleep ritual every night: lulling music, warm bath, chamomile tea.

Foods that induce sleep are milk, avocados, bananas, cheese, turkey, yogurt—foods with high levels of the amino acid tryptophan. Eat these when trying to get to sleep, not when you're trying to be alert.

A hot bath can make you sleepy by raising core body temperature. Cold wakes you up; warmth puts you to sleep. (Wear socks to bed! It is impossible to get to sleep with cold feet!) It's the rise in body temperature, and then the cooling off, that causes drowsiness.

16. tired

getting rest

● The first step for beating insomnia is checking physical comfort: Is your bedroom calm, cozy, dark, and noise-free? Is your bed comfortable?

Our bodies are cued by light. If artificial light has disrupted your sleep patterns, you may need to experiment with getting back to more natural light transitions. Try creating a very dark bedroom without night-lights, and connect a low-level bedside light to a timer that turns it on an hour before you usually wake up, for a more natural "dawn."

● *If you're tossing and turning, you need to relax. Tense up all your muscles, hold, then let go. Start with your feet: tense them, then let them go limp. Work your way up your body. Allow fingers, shoulders, and jaw to relax.*

When you are keyed up and excited about something that's happening the next day, or wracked by worries, it's hard to fall asleep. Make a deliberate ritual of leaving your concerns behind as you enter the bedroom: Write down your problems and plans for tomorrow and leave the list on a table downstairs. Tell yourself you'll deal with them tomorrow.

17. BORED

finding inner resources

If you don't feel like doing anything, do it wholeheartedly! Sit around the house and watch mind-numbing daytime TV for a few hours. Curl up with a really trashy novel or magazine. Wallow in the boredom. Do absolutely nothing—we all need time to veg out completely once in a while and regroup before the next adventure. The world is full of magical things waiting for you to come to your senses. Eventually you'll get tired of boredom and be ready to open yourself to life again.

Life is not dull; there are only dull people.

Is there a whole empty weekend stretching ahead? This is the perfect opportunity to do something time-consuming: Make jam. Bake bread. Paint your bedroom.

Maybe boredom is your mind's way of avoiding a big issue. Do you switch off when confronted with things you fear? (Things you fear can intrude on you in a very subtle way. Reading the obituary of someone your age, for example, might remind you of your own mortality.) Like depression, boredom can be a mood your mind hides behind so you don't have to feel emotions you don't want to let yourself feel.

Nothing ever happens in your life? Make it happen! An adventure is anything you've never tried before, even if it's something small. See where the 509 bus ends up, become a redhead, speak with a French accent for a whole day.

"What'll we do, Mom? We're so bo-o-red..."

You'll do your kids a lifelong favor if you encourage them to make their own fun rather than rely on pre-packaged junk-food-type fun like TV. This kind of fun will always get boring, eventually, but the kind of activities they bring something of themselves to won't. When kids are bored, don't try to get them to do something virtuous, like tidy their room.

Suggest they:
- ▶ Bend wire into different shapes and see what kind of bubbles form when blown through them.
- ▶ Come up with the best knock-knock joke.
- ▶ Make a batch of cookies.
- ▶ Teach the dog a useless new trick.
- ▶ Paint each other's faces with makeup.

Make a list of all the things you absolutely don't feel like doing. Without meaning to, you'll come up with a few things that you actually wouldn't mind doing at all.

Been everywhere and done everything?
You need to feel like a beginner again in a new job or new surroundings.

18. grateful

> "Writing is translation, and the opus to be translated is yourself."
>
> —E. B. White

Keep a journal; it's a great pressure valve for emotions. It's your stage. Tell the audience exactly how you feel about things in explicit detail, how maligned and hassled you are. Every day you have a chance to curse everyone, to rant and rave, to let go of anger and frustration on the pages.

Why be grateful for things? Because if you don't recognize something good when it happens, you can't let it help you or make you happy; you can't learn from it.

Writing isn't just for would-be novelists. There are many different reasons to write, and there's no need to form all your thoughts into lyrical, poetical sentences. In a journal your writing is a way of talking to yourself. Essayists write to put down opinions they already hold—a journal can help you find out what you are thinking and make your insights more conscious and lasting and easier to evaluate. It's a way of more fully owning your own experience. Writing can make hopes more real and fears easier to deal with. You can discover your dreams and define your goals—the first step in making things happen. (Should I spend a year in Rome? Get married? Become a vet?)

Use a journal that has a beautiful cover,
and you'll be motivated to write often.

What we put our attention on grows stronger in our lives. Don't just focus on difficulties and failures in your journal. Every night, write down at least one nice, positive thing that happened during the day: a compliment, time out to look at the clouds, a kindness shown you. Make it a habit to find at least one thing to be grateful for—nothing is too small to write down. These tiny blessings make great reading on days when everything seems bleak. And if you write the good things in green ink, you'll know it's time to give yourself more treats when there hasn't been much green ink for a while.

Accept as a gift whatever the day brings.

Rather than concentrating on how bad things are, focus on the fact that they could be much worse. Psychiatrists call this downward comparison. You think of someone worse off not to gloat, but to gain a new perspective on your situation and new understanding about how to cope.

19. RUSHED

time pressure

Have you ever considered that you may not actually be *allowing* yourself to have free time? Leaving things until the last minute builds up high-adrenaline anxiety levels that can be stimulating and addictive. We choose to accept pressure and responsibility. To have time to relax, you have to be able to feel okay about relaxing. No time management technique will help if you feel guilty when you take time off to play.

> Put a dollar value on your time. You'll stop wasting it, and you'll know whether it makes more sense to hire someone else to do things you don't like doing.

Too busy to enjoy life? Make sure your activity reflects your true values. When most of your time is spent doing things that reflect what you really love and believe in, what really counts in your life, life will feel worthwhile rather than rushed. Put your time where your heart is.

At work, it's vital to know what your boss sees as being top priority. You might believe **quantity** is important, while her goal is **quality**. If you are in sync, you can achieve a lot more than if you are both following your own agenda.

To help you be flexible in terms of time available versus amount of detail you need to bring to a task, try to get an overall view of what is necessary. In the same way as you would flip through a how-to book to evaluate its contents before you decide which chapters you need to read, try to "see" the whole project, its component parts, and how they relate to one another in your mind's eye. Get the big things in place before you start obsessing about the little things.

The frantically busy person is sometimes running from thoughts he doesn't want to face.

If you wait until you have "enough time," the laundry will always come before writing the novel.

Make molehills out of mountains: Break up the big things into manageable little chunks and decide, with a day planner, when to do them. Delegate what you can.

Sometimes it's more important to be connecting with people than it is to be doing things.

You set the agenda for your life. Schedule *pleasure.*

Prioritize by asking: Will it matter a year from now? What will happen if I do nothing?

20. Overheated

cooling down

Savor the simple congenial joys of warm weather:

use the built-in excuse
Waste the day at a double feature in an air-conditioned cinema; research cryogenics; drive with the top down; wear tanned legs instead of stockings.

frozen treats Whatever your favorite food, see what it tastes like frozen solid—start with frozen grapes and frozen Mars bars.

being abandoned
Slide an ice cube along someone's spine; wear a sarong; watch a movie outside under the stars; taste-test all the gelato flavors at your local gelateria to find your absolute favorite.

cool cuisine Use cooling spices: lemongrass, mint, and coriander; make tzatziki, the Greek dip that combines cucumber and yogurt; eat sushi, key lime pie, and watercress; take longer than necessary to inspect the contents of the refrigerator.

beach therapy Can't get to the beach? Pour a cup of sea salt into the bath as the faucets fill it with cool water—sea salt contains magnesium, zinc, and potassium, which relax the muscles. That's why a swim in the ocean feels so good.

tasting summer Farmstand lettuce; real lemonade; the first taste of fresh raspberries, corn, tomatoes, and watermelon; slushy drinks with little paper umbrellas in them.

being outside Find open-air concerts, sand castle contests, carnivals; take ferry rides; window-shop while licking an ice cream; swing on the swings; bury your feet in the sand.

the freedom Getting caught in the warm summer rain of a sudden late-afternoon thunderstorm when it doesn't matter how you look; sparklers for the Fourth of July; twenty minutes in front of a fan with a cool drink and a book set in the Arctic.

doing silly things Wear a flower in your hair or a moisturizer with sparkles on your body; dab neon-colored zinc oxide on your nose; run through the garden sprinkler.

being childish Host a watermelon-eating contest; cannonball off the high diving board; decorate your flip-flops; make a daisy chain; find cheap, silly sunglasses.

summer city torpor The way curtains at an open window billow lazily; the sounds of a ball game on a passing radio; melting sidewalks.

surreal summer twilights the chirp of crickets, mosquitoes, fireflies; meteor showers and falling stars.

letting loose Wear loud Hawaiian shirts; sleep naked; run after the ice cream truck or barefoot in the park.

What is essential to make you feel good and look your best? Shiny, clean hair? Lots of sleep? Good shoes? If these make you feel good, they are important.

21. frumpy
looking good

Keep only the clothes that make you feel great. Ordinary clothes stay ordinary no matter what you pair them with, but outstanding clothes elevate a whole outfit and make you feel outstanding, too. If you get rid of the nonwonderful, then the wonderful has a chance to shine.

"It is only shallow people who do not judge by appearances."
—Oscar Wilde

Dress in a similar way to people with whom you want to develop a rapport, to make them feel you are one of them, a member of the club. That's what uniforms do: de-emphasize individuality and make people feel part of a team.

Clothes and grooming show how you feel about yourself but also determine how you feel about yourself—if you are feeling down, washing your hair or putting on nice clothes can help.

One way of deciding what to wear is dressing for the response you want. Think about who you want to appear to be, and how you want others to feel about you. You can dress not only for success but to annoy, to amuse, to look like an intellectual. Dress to convey the subliminal message you want received—clothes have symbolism.

> "The sense of being well-dressed gives a feeling of inward tranquility which religion is powerless to bestow."
> —R. W. Emerson

Yes, of course, you can wear whatever you like, and people shouldn't judge you by your clothes. But what else do they have to go by, before they've spent any time with you? That's why it is important that the costumes in a movie are just right—they reveal so much about character. If people get the wrong idea about who you are, it may be that the packaging is misleading. New acquaintances assume that clothes are a mirror of what's inside. Make it work in your favor.

Time-saving chic: Have an accessory that is your trademark—many clattering bracelets, your grandmother's ring, a silver watch chain worn as a necklace—that you wear all the time, even to bed.

If you wouldn't want anyone to describe you as (*insert adjective*), don't wear clothes that could be described as (*insert same adjective*).

To take up a good
habit, hook it onto
something you
already do
regularly.

22. SLEAZY
bad habits

To get rid of a bad habit, like nail-biting:

1. Ask yourself how you'll feel when you've given it up. Keep that feeling in sight; it's your motivation.

2. Become aware of those crucial few seconds just before you put your fingernail to your mouth. Only when you can anticipate what you're going to do will you be able to stop.

Backsliding is an
opportunity to figure
out the weakest link
in your plan. Learn
from what
happened; don't
criticize yourself.

3. Recognize the situation or chain of events that makes you tense, what you tell yourself at these times, and what emotion is associated with the habit. Whenever you find yourself nibbling, ask, why am I doing this? And why right now? What am I getting out of it—a release of tension, a sense of being in control?

Begin behaving like
the person you want
to be, no matter how
awkward it feels.

4. Create a competing response, something to turn your attention to when you feel the emotion—

You must really, really want to make the change you say you want. Sounds simple, but sometimes there's a hidden benefit from bad behavior—if you gave it up people might stop feeling sorry for you, for example, or you might have to take on more responsibility, or perhaps there'd be no excuse, then, for not improving other areas of your life.

· ·

preferably a good habit such as massaging the acupressure point between your thumb and index finger. Rehearse mentally so you'll know what to do when the impulse to bite your fingernails comes.

5. Remind yourself—put a Post-It note on the mirror, or link the good behavior with a symbol you keep bumping into.

6. Every time you look at your fingernails, visualize them long and unbitten; picture having achieved your goal as if it were real. (Your body won't cooperate unless your mind knows what it wants. But don't bully yourself.) When these tactics start working, you get the reward of results: Admire your new nails and use those positive feelings to motivate yourself further.

Slip-ups are normal—that's why pencils come with erasers.

Be as conscientious about keeping promises to yourself as you would be to someone you admired.

Be self-centered enough to care about your body by looking after it.

Physical pain means something is wrong with your body. Emotional pain means something is wrong with your thinking, or that your thinking is at odds with what's happening. Constant crabbiness is the equivalent of ignoring an ache in your body—you need to get help.

To begin with, aim to feel just a little less bad. Maybe calling a friend will achieve that. Next, build on those slightly improved feelings little by little to get a bit more balance in your outlook. Anything that prods you to think more optimistic thoughts is a good idea.

Feeling blue has been described as "anger without the enthusiasm." Psychologists say that depression is anger turned inward. Maybe you're angry about something but are cutting off those angry feelings for some reason.

Humans automatically "self-medicate" when they feel bad, in an attempt to bring themselves back into balance. (Sometimes we're aware of what we're doing and sometimes we're not.) When you're feeling down, avoid self-medicating in a way that will leave you feeling worse later (such as with alcohol or overeating).

Try to get some sunshine, fresh air, and laughter soon.

23. despondent

lose the blues

• Chronic, low-grade depression is like a psychological head cold, or living through an overcast day that goes on and on. If you've been depressed for years—functioning, but with feelings of helplessness and hopelessness, and not able to get pleasure out of life—you may have a condition known as dysthymia. The first step to recovery is getting a complete checkup to rule out any physical illnesses that might be causing the depression.

What really works for chasing the blues away? Doing something positive to solve any problems you have. Do something you do well, to remind yourself you're pretty damn good, in spite of everything. What doesn't work? Blaming your bad mood on others.

Sometimes (but only some-times) a really vigorous, all-out attack on housework is an antidote for melancholy.

"There are no cures—only the possibility of turning hysterical misery into everyday unhappiness."
—Sigmund Freud

Our words influence how we think, and how we think influences how we feel. If you keep talking about how awful everything is, you'll keep *thinking* how awful everything is and you'll keep *feeling* awful. Depression is a thinking disorder. To feel better, it's really important to start talking to yourself in a positive way.

People often use criticism to keep others under control and to make themselves feel superior.

If criticism is designed to hurt you, the person dishing it out has her own problems that have little to do with you.

24. chastised

deflecting criticism

Criticism means someone didn't like something you did—not necessarily that he or she doesn't like who you are. Next time someone condemns you, especially if he mixes abuse with the criticism, don't react. Step out of yourself, imagine you are watching what is happening from somewhere else in the room. If you get angry, take yourself away and come back later. Separate what was said from the way it was said. Listen carefully, ask for clarification, and repeat back what you think you've heard. Acknowledge the extent to which you agree. This way you'll be able to evaluate the words calmly, decide whether they are justified, and know what you should do.

Every time we're rejected and criticized, it calls to mind all the ghosts of past rejection and criticism.

"The girl who can't dance says the band can't play."
—*Yiddish proverb*

You don't have to accept criticism of yourself, just your behavior. Sometimes you can educate the person disparaging you and point out the difference. Tell her that you'd find it easier to accept criticism about what you did rather than who you are.

Our instinct is to argue with someone who criticizes us, but arguing usually leaves each side even more convinced of his or her own view. Instead, sift through what was said for the feedback that is valuable to you and ignore everything else about the message.

Family members often feel they have a right to say something negative. If someone close to you constantly criticizes under the guise of caring for you, the way to deal with it is to agree in part with the criticism. This should stop the message if you do it often enough. For example, to the comment "You'd look so much better with short hair," reply calmly, "Yes, short hair does look good on some people." Just keep agreeing when someone wants to change you or says you screwed up. This takes away a person's power.

If nobody ever says anything bad about you, you are definitely not living up to your full potential!

25. responsive
the art of listening

Mirroring the body language of a person to whom you are speaking feels phony, but it's what people do, unconsciously and naturally, when they have rapport with each other. They echo each others' gestures, rate of speech, and emotional state—almost like a dance. But if you do this artificially, it means you are more aware of your own body than what the other person is saying. And if someone thinks you are mimicking them, they won't trust you. In fact, deliberately mismatching someone's body language (by looking away, for example) is what we do when we *don't* want to talk.

You'll get much closer to the people in your life if, instead of merely hearing speech without absorbing it, you really listen. That means trying to understand and assess what people say. It can be difficult because we process words much faster than others speak. Our minds start wandering away from the conversation, especially when distractions are present. Real listening is being involved. To listen well, you have to show that you are there for someone by your eye contact, posture, tone of voice, and reactions. Maintain an attentive silence. Don't ask too many questions, but keep a person talking by making encouraging sounds. If you stay out of the way, you can more easily discover someone's feelings.

Get someone talking by noticing her mood. ("You look happy today!")

You also have to be open to the values and beliefs of the speaker—otherwise, you'll hear only what you expect to hear. Let someone know you've heard them by paraphrasing, and by reflecting back their mood and content, in the same way you'd repeat a telephone number to make sure you have it right. This is necessary because neither of you will be aware that a misunderstanding exists if it isn't checked.

If you are talking to someone across a desk, you are less likely to connect. To get closer mentally, get closer physically. Crouch down to talk to a child or someone in a wheelchair.

Closed questions are ones that require only a yes or no answer—use them when you want to clarify facts. Open questions (what, why, when, how, where, who) encourage someone to speak freely.

Often, the way a message is delivered can tell you more about how a person feels than its content. People often talk to relieve feelings of tension, or to express excitement or enthusiasm about something—the words aren't important.

26. childish
flow equals fun

"It's never too late for a happy childhood."
—Gloria Steinem

Have you ever looked forward to just relaxing and doing absolutely nothing on vacation, then been surprised that you felt bored and empty just sitting around? True happiness comes when you're concentrating, completely and effortlessly, on something that calls for active participation. Take juggling, for example—a test of skill with a clear goal with immediate feedback on how you're doing—it's a totally absorbing activity. The way you feel when you do something where your skills are in perfect balance with the challenges has been called "flow." The luckiest people get a feeling of flow from their job, but you can also get it, as children do, from play.

Rekindle your childhood curiosity. Ask How Come? and What If? and Why Not? and let yourself be surprised at how you feel and act.

Children start out as individuals, looking at the world through first-time eyes. But their unique, creative way of thinking gets stifled by school, their desire to fit in, and the need to conform and to be in charge of their feelings. But now that you've learned those necessary lessons, you can let go again and be spontaneous and frivolous and crazy. You can take time out to be a kid, and let go for the right reasons, for the sheer pleasure of it. You'll get in touch with an essential, unique part of yourself again.

Learn something new. Discover hidden enthusiasms; take a class in anything that sounds even vaguely interesting. The mind of the beginner is empty, ready to accept, open to all possibilities. That's a great attitude to bring to a class, and to life, too.

Go toy shopping. Stock up on bubbles, Silly String, colored chalk (for drawing on the driveway), Slinkies, windup toys. *Not for the kids, for you.*

Delight in the absurd.

Children know that happiness signifies something important.

"You can learn many things from children. How much patience you have, for instance."
—Franklin P. Jones

Stop whatever kind of exercise you're currently doing and take up tap dancing.

Jump rope; make a macaroni necklace and wear it; put glow-in-the-dark star stickers all over your bedroom ceiling.

Find your favorite childhood candy; teach a baby to blow raspberries; read the Sunday comics before you turn to the news section.

The unrelenting stimuli of modern life can drain energy. Try shutting out what you can in your immediate environment (with headphones, for example) and make your surroundings more comfortable with soothing things to look at and friendly furniture. Just getting more in control—tossing out all the newspapers you'll never catch up with, making a list of chores, clearing your desk—helps as well.

The amount of sleep and exercise you're getting, your diet, and your health are all connected. A lethargic mood can often be traced back to one of these variables. And energy ebbs and flows in daily, monthly, and seasonal waves. Time of day really makes a difference to how we are feeling—most people's energy is at its peak in the early afternoon. Know when your best times are and try to schedule the things that take more energy to be done at the times you actually are most energetic.

On a day you need lots of energy, eat small, frequent meals rather than fewer heavy ones; remember to stop and take a few slow, deep breaths from time to time; and get up from what you are doing every hour or so and do something completely different— even a tiny change in routine makes you more productive. If you've been sitting at the computer, water the plants. If you've been making dinner, sit down with a magazine.

27. drained

getting energy

Your body has to work twice as hard when it's not aligned properly. Are you sitting up straight?

Emotionally draining people can make you feel tired. Appreciate people who know how to be joyful and make you laugh.

If you've lost your energy suddenly or if you feel tired all the time, get to a doctor for a physical.

"Life begets life. Energy creates energy. It is by spending oneself that one becomes rich."
—Sarah Bernhardt

Take a minute to smell the oranges—citrus and mint help keep you alert. Spritz a little scent on your wrist for a quick lift.

Take every day of vacation you have earned at work.

Fresh fruit juice gets absorbed into your body immediately, gets you energized fast, and is better than coffee and candy. And remember that even a little dehydration can make you feel tired.

Feelings are what give you energy. Acknowledge them, even if they are ones of lethargy, numbness, and depression.

Ask someone to tell you a joke.

28. affectionate

ways to say "I love you"

Feed and encourage that part of his soul that rarely gets nourished. Rejoice in his successes, recognize his strengths.

Look forward to the end of the romantic stage of your relationship! Falling in love is feeling the delight we had when our mothers mirrored our every expression lovingly. Once you each stop seeing the other as the "missing" part of yourself and idealizing complete fusion, the saner you'll be. After the romantic stage comes the companionship stage, when the relationship itself becomes more important, and you recognize your lover as the flawed but worthy human being he is—and you recognize that of yourself, as well.

No matter how successful a person is, he wants to matter more to his partner than to anyone else in the world. Tell him why he matters to you.

Make anything edible (sandwiches, cheese slices, pie-crust tops) heart-shaped with a heart-shaped cookie cutter.

Remember the shared enthusiasms that brought you together.

Listen to his heartbeat.

Recognize and appreciate the essential him. What lights up his face with joy? It may not be exactly what you think it is. He may spend hours setting up his computer to do complicated things, but the computer isn't the essential him. The essential him is fascinated by putting systems together.

Choose to see the good in those you love.

Each of us places more importance on one sense than the others. If he's a tactile person, he needs to be given hugs. If the spoken word resonates most with him, he needs to hear compliments. If he's sight-oriented, he needs to receive gifts. If he doesn't need any more objects in his life, give him perishable things like a song from the jukebox, or fresh-squeezed orange juice in the morning, or a trip to the town where he grew up. Express love in ways that are important to him, not you.

If she's the most important person in your life, are you treating her as if she is, making her feel cherished, important, and respected? If she's not, why aren't you with the person who is?

It's through what you do—your actions—that people know your relationship with them takes precedence over anything else. Show up at the airport when he doesn't expect to be met. Massage his feet while he's watching TV. Find a way to get the impossible-to-get tickets to the sporting event that means the most to him.

If someone has an "attitude," you should deal with it as you would if you were being verbally manipulated. Tell him that you feel you are being coerced and clearly state your own boundaries—what you will and won't do. Then try not to let his mood infect you.

29. **sulky**
self-pity

"Self-pity in its early stages is as snug as a feather mattress. Only when it hardens does it become uncomfortable."

—Maya Angelou

Sulking is withholding—withholding your emotions, speech, or companionship. It's an attempt to punish someone or to try to make her care by demonstrating your unhappiness without putting it in words. When we withdraw emotionally, we can effectively hurt a person who is afraid of our anger or who has a great need for our approval.

If you feel sulky, you need to put your anger into words. Children sulk, or have "an attitude," when their parents won't let them express their feelings.

Things happen that need attention. Trees fall into neighbors' yards, machines wear out, books go missing, life isn't fair. Thinking that things "should" go the way you want, that people "should" act a certain way, and feeling sorry for yourself when they don't, is a way of not facing up to what has to be done. You have to learn to cope with what happens and with your own feelings about what happens.

Feelings of self-pity are based on the assumption that one is helpless. Trying to make others feel guilty reinforces this belief. But there is always something you can do.

If you sulk in order to dump your bad feelings onto someone else and make you feel in control, you'll keep doing it. But it is a manipulative method of changing someone else's behavior, and you end up doing long-term damage to yourself. Chronic sulking means you're spending all your energy trying to make others feel bad. You get in the habit of blaming them not only for everything that goes wrong, but also for your own feelings of frustration and tension. You close yourself off from joy and happiness.

Try to let little annoyances slide by you. There are so many things that are not worth feeling resentful about.

Sulking is effective only when you spend enough time with others for them to be aware of your unhappiness. Eventually they will leave and all you'll be left with is your own misery.

No one can argue if you say, "I find it disruptive when you—" But if you say, "You are disturbing everyone," that can be disputed. Describe what you saw, how you felt about it and the consequences that had a negative impact, and what you would have preferred. If possible, let the other person suggest a change; encourage him to make a plan to change his behavior.

Letting someone know that doing a certain thing would produce a positive outcome is far more productive and motivating than complaining and pointing out the problem when he fails to do something. Say, "If you put the sheets in the dryer, we'll be able to make up the bed before we go," rather than "Can't you see the washing machine has stopped?"

Ask for better results, don't expect a change in outlook. You can't change a person's invisible attitudes, preferences, values, and beliefs—but you can ask her to change the part that shows, you can ask her to modify what she does.

It helps to know what motivated someone's bad behavior. If you want to influence someone, show her that what you are suggesting will benefit her.

Phrases like, "How many times do I have to tell you?" only demonstrate your failure at communication.

30. influencing others
PERSUASIVE

To criticize someone's behavior without angering him, choose a time when he'll be receptive and talk to him in a private, nondistracting environment with a calm, relaxed, friendly demeanor. If the person feels blamed or threatened or misunderstood, he will react with hostility and be unlikely to change his ways. If you criticize in the midst of a conversation about other things, the impact is more diluted than if you meet to discuss just one problem. Always focus on the behavior, not the person; the performance, not the performer. Don't say, "You are too quiet" but "I need everyone to give their opinions at our meetings." Don't exaggerate—try to be as factual as possible. Say, "You have been late six times this month" rather than, "You're never on time."

After you've asked someone to change her behavior, get her to repeat back your request to make sure she's understood. Words can have different meanings for different people, and listeners can be distracted or can color their understanding with their own preconceptions.

Even with family members, don't use blaming phrases. Don't say, "You make me feel . . . ," say, "When you do that, I feel . . ."

Pare a problem down to its essentials or enlarge the parameters. You want to be with the kids, but have to go shopping? Hire someone to do the shopping, instead of a babysitter. Trying to decide whether to go to a party you don't think you'll enjoy? Ask yourself instead: How can I have the best time on Saturday night wherever I am?

31. inefficient
finding practical solutions

If you are having a problem trying to understand something new, or describing how you're feeling, try searching for an analogy or metaphor that captures the essence of the issue. (Your living room isn't a theater, but if you imagine how it would work if it were, you might come up with a better place to put the TV.) This is how the brain gets a handle on things: by connecting what is unknown to what is known. Metaphors can also put problems in a new light and give you new ways of thinking about them.

You don't have to have a high IQ to have brilliant ideas; you just need to train yourself to think in a different way.

Try coming up with little improvements to make your life easier; it's good practice. What made you frustrated today? How could you fix it?

If you're trying unsuccessfully to solve a problem, try not taking it seriously. Humor and creativity come from the same place in our brains. They require the same kind of thinking and get a similar response. How do cartoonists come up with funny ideas for cartoons on a regular basis? They keep testing combinations of words and drawings that are not usually associated, until they come up with a funny juxtaposition. Good ideas can be created the same way: by making unexpected mental connections, combining concepts that are not normally combined, and using ridiculousness to look beyond the expected, right way of doing things.

How can the negative aspect of a problem become the positive aspect? (Post-It notes were created by chemists who inadvertently made a glue that wouldn't stick.)

Work backward: Visualize the end result. How did that happen?

Define your problem. Carry a notebook and write down anything you see that relates to it. Ask stupid questions. Look for random stimuli in everything you read or hear. Totally immerse yourself in finding a solution.

How would your hero or role model solve your problem?

love what you do

The more you know yourself, the easier it is to know the right work for you. What parts of your job fully engross you? What do you get so involved in that you lose track of time? When does the day drag? What activities do you always have time for, no matter how busy you are? Which abilities are you using then? Do you prefer being part of a team or working alone? What kinds of statistics always stay in your mind? During the day, note what you enjoy doing, and why. Notice what your mind enjoys thinking about, what tasks your hands do naturally, what's easy to concentrate on. Which days are you just getting by; which work makes your soul sing? When are you at your most resourceful?

Who is earning money doing what you'd love to do?

"The significant business of your life is alive and well, awaiting discovery, within your very soul."

—Marsha Sinetar,
To Build the Life You Want,
Create the Work You Love

Establish transition routines to ease you into and out of work. Before you leave the office, write down a list of priorities for tomorrow. Leave the list at the office and forget about it until then.

Are you confusing yourself with your job?

Is the work you're doing smaller than your soul?

The most stressful jobs have responsibility but no authority. Does that describe your job, and is it worth the high blood pressure and heart attacks that stress leads to?

When you know what your essential nature is, you can use your job to express it. You'll be able to think of yourself as someone who helps people, or who keeps politicians honest, or who is an inspiring boss.

If your job doesn't feel like the perfect friendship, what would make it so? It may be something as simple as having a table light on your desk for easier reading, or a plant on the filing cabinet, or getting yourself a more comfortable mouse for the computer. Or it may be a way of bringing your skills to your job in a new way—finding a better method of doing something, thinking of your boss as a customer rather than an authority figure, working with people or ideas rather than things.

Talk to the people who benefit from your work. You'll realize how valuable you are.

33. *kindhearted*

comforting friends

Be a friend, not a therapist. The words you use aren't important; a grieving person doesn't need you to say anything in particular. The real comfort comes from knowing a friend is present during the pain.

Grief is not only emotionally but physically exhausting as well. Encourage a grieving person to exercise, to eat regularly, and to look after herself.

Grieving people are often so dazed they don't know what kind of help they need. Don't just say, "Call me if there's anything I can do," or "Let us know if you need something," which puts the whole burden on someone who is probably finding it difficult to cope. If you have expertise in an area where your friend needs assistance, offer it. Or look around to see how you might help and make a specific offer that the bereaved person can simply say yes or no to, such as taking the kids for the weekend, putting an announcement in the newspapers, sitting by the phone to list everyone who calls, helping with logistics. But don't do anything without asking or be too intrusive. Don't offer to do something if you don't intend to follow up.

What usually comforts the bereaved most are memories of the deceased and recollections about him or her, to know his or her life meant something. Remember anniversaries, holidays, and birthdays—they'll be difficult. Good friends continue to make comforting gestures after the first awful weeks.

If a friend asks disturbing questions ("What's the use of going on?"), he is not looking for a logical, direct answer. He needs to explore his feelings and would benefit by talking to a therapist. Try to work out the real purpose of such questions.

Write a note rather than send a commercial card.

Don't try to distract a distraught person because the grief is painful for you to witness, and don't make her put on a brave face so as not upset you. Don't push her to talk if she's not ready. Grief doesn't adhere to a timetable. Let your friend take her own time. It's not your place to tell someone else how she should feel sorrow.

Initial reactions to a great loss are usually anger, denial, or numbness. A bereaved person can forget momentarily that someone close has died and can resent others as they return to their normal routines. You may not feel you can help a friend through these stages. Just be there and listen.

We are all misfits. We all have disabilities—physical or emotional—that we grapple with throughout life, just by virtue of being alive.

Do you come home from your demanding job and yell at the dog? This is displacement. It's not the dog you are angry at. If you go to the gym and put the energy of your anger into exercise, that's displacement too, but a better kind.

The mentally healthy individual confronts what threatens him rather than projecting his fears onto other people. (Projection is when we decide that someone else embodies a trait we're afraid of facing up to in ourselves.)

Be curious rather than condemning. Think, "Why does she feel the need to do that?" rather than, "Why is she doing that to me?"

Strange people are the spice and pickles and chutney of life. (And believe it or not, they think you're a little weird, too!)

Feel invisible and ignored? Lucky you! Invisibility gives you power—the power to be yourself, the freedom to do as you please, to not be defined by other people's opinions.

You can dislike what a person does, you can disagree with his thinking, and you can be uncomfortable with what he feels, but you won't gain anything if you judge or condemn him. Everyone is a collection of strengths and weaknesses.

34. disadvantaged

disabilities and prejudice

Prejudice is fueled by misunderstanding. A man says, "Excuse me" in order to pass a deaf woman who doesn't move because she hasn't heard. The man pushes past anyway; the deaf woman is annoyed at his rudeness. Both are irritated because both jumped to erroneous conclusions. To do your part in eliminating misunderstanding, make your thinking more visible to others whenever possible. Find out how others arrived at their preconceptions rather than challenging them.

Belonging to a group satisfies basic psychological needs: the need to be with others and to develop a sense of identity. The more we think well of our group, the better we feel about ourselves. But comparison leads to prejudice and discrimination.

If you have a disability, you own it. You can help others who also have it. You can share all the coping mechanisms you've found with children who have it. You can make jokes about it.

35. solicitous

giving advice

If someone says, "It was awful, but I'm okay," but you know they are not, say, "I'd hate it if that happened to me. It would make me angry and upset." This lets the other person know that you can accept anger or resentment, and will not be shocked and horrified at his feelings.

Even though you may not be a professional therapist, there is a lot you can do to ease a friend's pain. Just listening to an emotional outpouring and being there for someone can be very helpful. Often a victim needs to go over and over an incident to try to explain to herself what happened.

Listen for the question really being asked— people seeking advice usually just want reassurance. They want to hear that it's okay to have the cat put to sleep, to leave their husband, or to buy the budget-blowing pair of shoes.

Ask the habitual complainer, "Now tell me what's going well in your life!"

Try to ease the pain rather than solve the problem for someone. Make him aware of his own strengths and abilities. Help but don't take control.

Don't make even lighthearted suggestions of revenge or domestic violence. Listen to character defamation of someone else's spouse, but never join in. Make a specific contract with a friend to stay in touch and call you if things get really bad.

Leave a person in pain with hope.

When counseling, try to put yourself and your desires aside. Focus on the needs of the person in pain. Don't tell anyone what to do or how to feel or give advice unless asked. It's not up to you to explain it all away. Don't say, "If I were you," because you're not. Instead, say, "Have you thought about . . . ?" Help a friend explore her options and clarify the issues. Try to find exactly where the pain lies, and what would be a relief or success from her point of view. Help her form achievable goals to get there.

Help someone be aware when they are mistakenly interpreting reality. If a friend says, "I really goofed; I'm stupid," turn his thinking around, remind him how competent he is.

Encourage reminiscing; it will remind someone that she's coped in the past and can cope again now.

36. Carefree
having fun

- For true happiness, aim for a steady diet of simple pleasures.

- **Keep a bottle of champagne in the refrigerator in case there's something to celebrate. And in case there's not.**

- Make a list of things you want to do before you're fifty.

- **Be eccentric: Host a cold-cereal dinner party featuring as many different brands as you can find. Or throw a junk-food potluck: Ask everyone to bring their favorite artificially colored candy or snack food.**

- Be silly: Sit inside the car as it goes through the car wash; dye the Dalmatian; have a favorite photo of yourself printed on the front of a T-shirt and wear it often.

> "Each of us needs to withdraw from the cares which will not withdraw from us."
> —Maya Angelou

- When was the last time you had a raucous girls' night out? Dress up. Drink cocktails. Laugh till your sides ache.

- **Get in touch with your inner teenager: Turn the volume way up. Own some red shoes, and wear them with anything but a matching red outfit.**

- Be spontaneous: Have spur-of-the-moment picnics; invent a salad; call dial-a-joke.

- **Don't let the filing or the ironing take precedence over taking your lunch to the park.**

- Sign up for something really scary: sky-diving, a theater group, the Big Dipper at the fair. The anxiety this generates will send any other problems right out of your mind.

- **Fun is life-affirming. It helps you remember that life is good.**

- Spend a whole day doing something you normally only let yourself do a little at a time.

- **Have an adventure every day, rather than just scheduling adventure once a year on your vacation. Change your morning routine: Treat yourself to breakfast out in an ethnic neighborhood. Get some face paints and a group of kids. Let a four-year-old decorate your face.**

- Make someone smile.

- **Go to open house inspections, visit mansions for sale or rent, imagine the fun of living in them. Now imagine all the cleaning and upkeep and organization necessary.**

- Visit some baby animals—at the zoo, at the pet store, on a *National Geographic* video.

- **Never care what anyone thinks. Buy a whole pile of tacky tabloids and trashy romances to read on the plane. When the person across the aisle stares, offer him one.**

> *"Happiness takes practice, as does anything else you want to be proficient at."*
> —John Kehoe, *The Practice of Happiness*

37. worthless

valuing yourself

"There is no value in life except what you choose to place upon it."

—Henry David Thoreau

Wanting to be famous is wanting approval, perhaps because you don't feel accepted by yourself.

Keep a record of how many times you apologize to other people during the day, and what you apologize for.

Behavior is often driven by the need to be accepted by others. The need to be liked can make you value the wrong things about yourself—the things you think others will like rather than the things you like about yourself.

Instead of always aiming to reach external status levels that depend on standards held by others, such as getting a raise or a college degree, try to accomplish internal goals, such as learning how to manage your negative thoughts or overcoming an irrational fear.

If your only way of pleasing your parents was by being useful—being worthy—you'll try to please others this way, too. But you may eventually resent them for not finding you inherently worthy.

You don't have to justify your existence to anyone.

♥

Your self-image is what you tell yourself about who you are. It's how you believe you should act to fit the way you see yourself. Your behavior and your reactions to what happens to you in life are dictated by your self-image. Your self-image is so much a part of you that even trying to change for the better can feel phony and pretentious if it doesn't fit in with how you see yourself.

Take notice when you belittle yourself by saying things like, "I never do this well," or, "You probably don't remember me," or, "This sounds crazy, but . . ." and try not to. We use phrases like these to avoid rejection—it's part of valuing others' opinions more than our own.

♥

If you grew up in a highly competitive family, everyone else becomes a rival. You can develop the mistaken belief that people will hate and ridicule you for any success you have.

You must discover for yourself your own worth and appreciate it. Get to really know yourself. Notice how you react in different situations, without judging whether your behavior was "right" or "wrong."

♥

Discover what you truly like or don't like, without comparing it to what you think you should like. Aim for quiet pleasure in being who you are.

When you are frustrated at work you have only three options: to change your attitude toward it, to change what's making the job unpleasant, or to change the job itself.

It's up to you to get what you want out of a job. Even if you loathe it, try to get something out of it. If you are learning and growing, think of it as a training program where you get paid.

Think back to the enthusiasm you had when you were first drawn to the kind of work you do now. Have you lost touch with that? Perhaps you love using the skills you have but are using them in the wrong environment. Perhaps you are a good lawyer, but hate courts. Or you are a teacher who'd rather work with adults than children. Think about how you can do what you love in an environment that's more stimulating.

Business is often not "fair." You can truly, really deserve a promotion and not get it. Salaries are based on what the market will bear. Don't measure success solely by your paycheck.

38. frustrated

problems at work

Job interviews: Go into them thinking *I'm here to help* rather than feeling like a child arranging to get an allowance in return for mowing the lawn. Employers want someone who is aware of the problems and challenges associated with the position and has ideas to solve them, ideas that they're eager to try out. Act as if you already have the job—show that kind of enthusiasm. Rewrite your résumé so it brings to life the skills you've mastered and the projects you've delivered. And at the end of the interview, ask for the job.

Instead of answering ads, think which local company you'd really like to work for. Point out to them how your skills are a perfect match with their organization. If it's a company you love, your appreciation will be genuine and irresistible, and they'll remember you when there is an opening.

If your job is repetitive, if you have little say over how you do tasks, if you get feedback only when something goes wrong, and if you never get the sense that your contribution counts, you probably hate what you're doing. What percentage of your day is spent happily? How do you feel at the end of the week? Does this job bring out your best qualities? What have you accomplished here that you can unashamedly boast about?

The family is our first, basic support group in society. Marriage should be a safe place to find sustenance. Support, defend, and protect each other in public, even if you disagree in private. An essential in a relationship is to make the other important, respected, and cared for. Your partnership should be something that helps you both through the little irritations of life, not a further irritation.

Couples who remain individuals, yet have a shared dream or shared hope, such as fixing up a home, or a united vision of creating a loving family, usually have good marriages.

Do you keep having the same relationship but with different people?

"No one has ever loved anyone the way everyone wants to be loved."
—Mignon McLaughlin

A successful relationship is not luck; it's an achievement. You have to focus on it, as you do on anything you want to enjoy.

If you're not getting through to him, it won't help to keep nagging. Frame complaints like this: "When you do A in situation B, I feel C" (Not, "You never . . .").

39. unloved

relationship woes

Men strive to solve problems by being practical; women by talking and sharing and giving advice. To men, being close is working or playing side by side; to women, it's talking face to face. Remember this and avoid the kind of misunderstandings that occur when he's thinking, "She must know I love her; I wouldn't spend all weekend building her a bookcase if I didn't love her," at the same moment she's thinking, "He spent all weekend outside building that damn bookcase to get away from me—he doesn't love me."

Start being the way you want the relationship to be. If you want a happy relationship, start being happy. If you want a loving relationship, be loving. Be true to your own values.

Do things for people out of love, not the fear of being unloved. As babies, we are helpless and learn to manipulate adults, but it's not healthy to have this same sense of helplessness, or a need to placate others, as an adult.

Relationship problems always seem to be the other person's fault—but what do *you* do that repeatedly creates the situation you don't like? Each partner should take 100 percent responsibility for his or her own life—no more and no less.

Do more of what works and less of what doesn't.

40. intelligent

staying smart

Smart people know how—and when—to use each side of their brains. The right hemisphere of the neo-cortex is the intuitive, spontaneous, experimental, imaginative, how-does-it-feel side; it deals with images, symbols, music, and fantasies. It's also the visual-spatial part that recognizes three-dimensional objects, looks for patterns and relationships, processes information about pictures, understands math, and coordinates motor skills. Boys, who are more visual and physical, are usually ruled by their right brains. The left hemisphere is the analytical, critical side that looks for logic and order and edits and evaluates and says, "Now w-a-i-t just a minute, is this practical? Let's look at this logically." It makes distinctions, categorizes, rationalizes, and judges. This side deals with speech and language, articulating emotion, and memorizing, and is usually larger in girls.

Keep your brain nimble: do crosswords, read the classics, take a class, solve the puzzles on the backs of cereal boxes.

The more you learn, the more you are able to learn. Learning actually promotes the growth of new neurons and prolongs the life of the ones you already have.

Those raised in Western societies are usually brought up to believe that rational, logical thinking is more reliable, but savvy people know to alternate right-brain thinking with left-brain thinking. Many writers, for example, write their first draft in right-brain mode, getting whatever comes to mind down on paper, then revise with their left-brain, editor side.

Most of the information you get every day comes from just your eyes and ears. To stay smart, do things that use the other senses and thus stimulate different areas of the brain. For example, have someone put a strange object into a bag. Without looking, explore the object inside with your fingers, then attempt to draw it.

How do you keep your brain functioning well, even in old age? Just as straining to lift weights strengthens muscles, your mind needs to be challenged regularly, to be forced out of its normal way of doing things. Go to a foreign movie, brush your teeth with the nondominant hand (the other hand from the one you normally use), or learn chess or a musical instrument. Varied, stimulating surroundings help keep your brain limber, too—an excuse to travel, even if just to a nearby town.

Ask your employees what they need from you to do their work well. Also ask them what motivates them. Often feedback is more important than money. Ideally, employees get satisfaction from doing good work, rather than praise from their boss.

41. bossy

managing people

The healthy business, like an individual's healthy mind, has all its different parts integrated, connected, and coordinated, and relates well to the outside world. The role of management is to remind every department in the organization of the importance of connecting well with the public.

To make sure everyone you work with keeps their word, ask, "Can I rely on you for that?"

Successful people are very clear about who they are, how they fit into their company's tribal culture, and what they want for themselves.

Why is it hard for you to delegate? Do you fear losing control? Or fear that others will assume you are expendable? Delegate responsibility, not just tasks. But stay involved. Lead, don't just point the way.

A manager's role is to translate the objectives and strategies of the company into actions, using the resources she has as effectively as possible. Those resources are mainly her staff, which is why she has to be good at motivating, guiding, and encouraging. Simply enforcing rules and regulations is not managing. Employees should be clear about what they're supposed to achieve.

Inconsistency in a leader is not conducive to morale. If you're mean, be mean all the time.

People tend to mirror childhood scenarios and treat their bosses the way they treated their parents when they were children, because that was their first experience of having someone more powerful supervising them. If a person's parents treated him with respect, he will respect his boss. This also explains the behavior of employees who are always seeking attention or approval.

Employees who seem to want to do the right thing but manage to annoy and provoke others and get out of doing what they are meant to do by "accidentally" messing up or forgetting could have a passive-aggressive behavior problem. These are people who bury their feelings of frustration and anger but display them in other ways, usually by manipulating others. They often have to be nagged relentlessly. They feel controlled and they resent it. A passive-aggressive employee would benefit from learning how to be assertive in a straightforward way.

42. **Argumentative**

resolving conflicts

To better understand where someone is "coming from" when he argues, it helps to know about a theory called **Transactional Analysis**, developed by psychiatrist Eric Berne. Berne outlines three ego states—parent, adult, and child—that people use, no matter what their age or status. When we are speaking in the **parent** state, we reflect rules we've been taught, and say authoritarian, stubborn, threatening, condescending things like, "You have no right to . . ." or "You must do it this way . . ." When we speak in the **adult** state, we are saying what we have thought out for ourselves; we reason, disclose, clarify, problem-solve, and say things like, "I see your point of view" and "I feel unhappy about this." When we speak from the **child** ego state, we react to our feelings about what is happening around us and whine, bargain, sulk, demand, and challenge, and say things like, "That's not fair!" "It's not my fault," and "I will if you will." When you recognize which state a person is talking from, you can concentrate on what he is saying rather than how he is saying it.

If the behavior of the other person is getting in the way, you could bring it to her attention by saying, "I can't think while you are yelling," or "If you use humor to get off-track, we won't get anywhere." This is called a content-to-process shift and gets discussion back to the point.

When trying to find a "win-win" situation and reach common ground, define the problem in terms of needs, not solutions. To discover needs, try to find why the person wants the solution she initially proposed. Once you understand the advantages that solution has for her, you have discovered her need. Instead of fighting over who gets to use the car, think how each of you can get where you want to go.

To de-escalate someone's defensiveness, reflect back to him his feelings and acknowledge his emotions. Don't get sidetracked reacting angrily to the content of a message that is expressed solely to upset you.

Avoid as much conflict as possible. Don't bother arguing with a person who doesn't have the power to deliver what you need. Ask yourself: What will I gain from avoiding this conflict? How would I like my relationship with this person to be in the future?

The gifts you give are symbolic of the emotions you have toward the recipient—so your first task is to identify what those emotions are. It's when you're feeling guilty or resentful about a relationship, for example, that you end up spending too much on the wrong thing.

When you care enough to send the very best, stop and think—think about the person who is receiving the gift. This means stepping into his life for a few minutes to get a feeling for what he needs. The perfect present affirms the recipient's sense of self.

43. Generous

the psychology of gift-giving

If you think you'll get ideas by strolling around the mall, you're approaching the problem the wrong way—you're trying to match up a "gift item" the stores want to get rid of with someone who probably has no need of that particular "gift item." Look beyond *your* emotional response to a gift—think about what the *recipient's* emotional response will be. If the gift is candy in a cute tin but she never eats candy, receiving this present won't rate too highly with her, no matter how adorable you consider the tin to be.

What kind of things does he get when he spends money freely and without hesitation? People don't appreciate gifts from their low-priority spending zones. The woman who resents having to buy a toaster but will happily spend half her paycheck on her twentieth pair of black pumps does not want to receive a kitchen appliance for her birthday.

A great present is a symbol of all the good feelings you have about your friend.

It's not only the thought that counts; it's the feelings that are communicated.

Write the card first. While you're still in the planning stages, put into words the emotions you are trying to express with your gift and it will be less likely to be misinterpreted. He's always there for you? Go beyond a plain "Happy birthday!" on the card. Write "This watch is to thank you for making time for me!"

Find the "why" behind the objects someone acquires for herself. What feelings does the purchase engender? Does she love cooking because she loves experimenting or because she loves entertaining? Sure, you could buy her more of what she already buys for herself. But finding the "why" is primarily a tool for understanding what means the most to a person. When you understand what motivates a person, you'll know the way to her heart.

✔ If you are making a presentation, know that despite all the work you put into the content, it's not what you say, but how you say it that counts. Audiences will listen to only about 30 percent of what you tell them and remember less than 10 percent of what they hear. And about 90 percent of your success depends on how you look and sound.

✔ Channel your nervous energy into gestures to underscore the meaning of the words—watch a TV personality to see how it's done.

✔ When you give a speech, you get to give a **gift** to the audience, to **wake** them up, to provide **new ideas** for them to think about. See it as an opportunity to shine, not fail. Concentrate on your message and getting it across, not your nervousness.

✔ Practice, practice, practice. Time spent in preparation always pays off, not only by improving your delivery but also by boosting your confidence.

✔ Never say, "I'm really nervous," when you are standing in front of a group. You don't look nervous.

44. Nervous
making speeches

✔ The tension you feel before a public performance can actually work for you, by giving you an edge. Anxiety and excitement are moods that are very similar. Use your nervousness as a positive force to charge you up. Do something physical before a speech, like walking up a flight of stairs. You don't want to be out of breath, just energized. At the lectern, an invisible exercise, like scrunching your toes, diverts some of the adrenaline. You don't want to shut off the tension, but you need to control it.

✔ **Visualization** helps a lot with stage fright. **Imagine** yourself, in vivid detail, making a very successful presentation. Remember back to a time when you were communicating effectively because you absolutely believed in what you were saying—the time you were persuading your parents to give you a bike, for example. And when you practice your speech in front of a mirror, "freeze-frame" the moments when you are making a point strongly, keep that **mental picture,** and see yourself re-creating it when you actually give the talk.

✔ Stage fright or performance anxiety is directly related to how judgmental you think others will be. Remind yourself that most audiences are sympathetic and want you to succeed. They don't mind watching you think on your feet as long as you remain in control by keeping your composure.

45. Coercive
getting your way

> If what you are asking is important to you, tell him that it is important.

To make a person do what you want, you have to make him want to do it for himself. Achieve this by relating it to his self-esteem needs—his desire to win approval and recognition and acceptance, his fear of rejection, his need to live up to a good reputation or prove his superiority. Aim to point out subtly to someone how he'll get these things by doing what you want him to do, perhaps by doubting that he has enough ability. You do this when you say to a kid: "I bet you can't put your toys away in five minutes."

To get someone to do something, give her the illusion of choice:

"Which part of this would you like to work on first?"

And assume that she will want to do the action you want her to do:

"When you do this you'll find that . . ."

 When someone won't see your viewpoint, sometimes altering your behavior completely helps: If you've been rational, become emotional; if you've been friendly, become serious.

We hook all our new learning and behavior onto what we have already experienced. We describe things in terms of what we already know: "It has a head like a bird but a body like a lion." That's why similes and metaphors are such an important part of our language. To encourage people to be open to your new idea, tell them about it in terms of what they already know. For example, use someone's own metaphors:

If she describes her job as a battle, use the same imagery to tell her to "make a truce" with her boss.

Know whether a person is motivated internally or externally and you'll be able to motivate him in a way he understands. Ask people how they know when they've made a delicious meal. Some will say, "Because it tastes great!" They motivate themselves. Others will say, "My family says it tastes good." They are motivated by what others think. If you want the first type of person to be on time, you'd say, "You know how important it is to be on time." To the second, you'd say, "I would really like you to be on time."

People will only do things that they see a benefit in doing. Point out that benefit.

Forgetting is not failure—our brains have actually evolved to forget details, to allow us to make life-saving, quick first impressions and snap decisions about new dangers. Information that is not used for a while fades to make way for more important data. The memories the brain considers important and worth retaining are typically those that have emotional significance (such as an unjust punishment when you were a child) or life-landmarks, such as our first kiss. Emotional memories, too, are crucial to decision-making and survival, because emotions are what spur us to action.

The more you learn, the more you are able to learn.

We recall most easily knowledge that's organized into a pattern, embedded in context, and meaningful.

Our mind makes images and processes them much faster than it does words. Recognizing faces was an early evolutionary necessity; remembering names uses a different part of the brain. We remember buildings better than street names and addresses, and we dream in pictures, not in words. So when you want to remember something, use your imagination to enhance the visual image to fantastic proportions. If you parked near a big red sign, imagine a huge container of red paint being poured over your car. To remember that this street is Locust Street, visualize a large locust sitting on top of each building. If you are trying to learn a poem, imagine yourself inside the imagery.

46. forgetful

memory help

How do you best learn a new subject? Do you prefer to memorize it? (You tend to remember things you see.) Or repeat the facts out loud? (Things you hear stay with you more easily.) Or write it down? (You need to be actively involved for information to stick.) When you know which method works best for you, you'll know your easiest way to learn. If you're studying French, for example, you'll know whether to choose tapes, draw yourself diagrams, or immerse yourself in a situation where only French is spoken— or whether to do all of them at once. An ideal learning situation is often one where all five senses are used together.

Remember lists of items by turning them into pictures that you connect in your mind's eye. Make the pictures as ridiculous and weird as possible and you'll remember them—and the list.

"Tell me and I'll forget. Show me and I may remember. Involve me and I'll understand."—Chinese saying

47. inhibited**inhibited**inhibited

feel all your feelings

- Life means experiencing strong emotions: fear, delight, sadness, joy. Don't try to run from the ones you don't like; experience them all. Even feelings like fear, guilt, and anger tell us things about ourselves, give us energy to change, and remind us what we consider important. Acknowledge painful emotions; recognize that they are part of you.

express

- By expressing your feelings, you let them go. If you try to act as if nothing happened, feelings will go underground—but they'll be expressed somehow: You'll snap at people, forget things you'd rather not remember, be late to places you don't want to go, and get tired when you don't want to do something. When these things happen, or you make a revealing Freudian slip, or have an apt memory or song or hunch come to you "out of nowhere," ask yourself why your unconscious is sending you this message.

experience

- **How are you camouflaging your pain? Common methods are to smother it, to abuse others with it, or to abuse ourselves.**

• When you are honest with yourself and can watch your behavior with interest rather than judgment, life becomes simpler. If you need to see your crazy relatives but can acknowledge to yourself that you don't really want to, you can figure out a way to make yourself happier about the obligation. Arrange to meet them at a movie or sports event so you will enjoy at least part of the get-together. Hire a car so you can go when you want to. Set your own limits. If you do things on your own terms in this way, you won't feel as if you are wasting time, you won't get irritated by people, and you'll enjoy life more.

• It's not painful emotions that are bad; it's denying you have them—and maybe you deny them because the family you grew up in disapproved of people displaying them. Children who learn honestly and fully to experience their real feelings become adults who are true to their own emotions. A teacher tells how colleagues were horrified when she allowed a child on his first day at nursery school to experience his grief and separation anxieties. If the teacher had said to the boy, "You're fine," and tried to distract him with toys, the child would have thought: "Something must be wrong with me. I'm scared and confused, but I'm told I'm not." Teaching a child to deny his emotion creates an adult who doesn't know what to do with his pain.

It's important to have good thoughts just before you go to sleep. Start a dream while you're still awake—go somewhere peaceful and soothing. Or try programming your unconscious to work on problems while you're asleep. (For this to work, you really have to want to know the answer.) Ask a specific question about something that's bothering you as you fall asleep, and repeat it over and over as you drift off. Write down whatever comes to mind first thing in the morning, in the present tense—keep a pen and paper next to your bed. If it makes no sense, try looking at it as a metaphor.

Recurring dreams usually indicate an unresolved problem in your life. As you drift off to sleep, visualize how you want the dream to end.

To make sense of a dream, try to remember as much as you can as soon as you awake, but don't take the story literally. Focus on how you felt, the texture of the dream, and how busy and complex it seemed, rather than the "plot." For example, if you dreamed you were in an empty house, analyze how you felt. Scared? Lonely? Is there any situation in your waking life in which you have the same feeling? Or try describing, as if to someone else, what the elements of the dream mean to you. For example, if you dreamed of the sea, think about what the sea represents to you—fear, fun, a place where you feel vulnerable? A dream can show several concerns at once.

48. Dreamy
unconscious emotions

Neurophysiologists think that dreaming is a way of digesting the day's experiences and consolidating memories: The mind puts together stray images and sensations into semi-plausible narratives. Freud believed that every dream is a repressed wish, and that all our dreams reflect some underlying unconscious desire. Today, psychiatrists believe dreams also indicate fears and needs that are too threatening to face when we're awake. To know what your unconscious is preoccupied with, be receptive to your dream's message and the emotions it evokes.

zzzzzz

Some dreams have obvious "meanings": Dreaming of being naked indicates concern about revealing something or feeling vulnerable; flying is about getting away from the limitations of everyday life; falling symbolizes loss of control. Trying but not being able to run from something represents a conflict between mind and body. Ask yourself, "Why am I having this dream now?"

Find an exercise option that's an outlet for emotion, that makes you feel better afterward—try belly-dancing or yoga or horseback riding—and learn to do it well for the fun of being good at it for the endorphin high, and to raise your energy levels.

The days you don't feel like exercising are the days it will do you the most good.

It's through our body that we know we're alive.

"Throughout their lives, women try to pummel their bodies into some phantom ideal shape that exists only with a lot of airbrushing. . . . I blame capitalism. . . . The consumer must constantly be in a state of anxious low self-esteem so that she will constantly buy lipsticks and girdles to make her feel cuter."—Cynthia Heimel, *If You Leave Me Can I Come Too?*

Being thin and beautiful really isn't what counts, it's believing you are. How you feel about yourself and your body shows in your body language. People who are comfortable in their own skin are incredibly attractive. If you believe you are sexy, you are sexy.

Who is more important to you—the latest Miss America, or the teacher who knew you'd succeed? Who gets more pleasure from her body—the sculptor whose gnarly hands are her tools, or the hand-model who lives in fear of a hangnail?

49. Graceless
body image

Cherish your body the way you would a battered, much-loved teddy bear. It's been through a lot with you, and makes you feel good. Who cares if it has a few quirks or is a bit the worse for wear? The idiosyncrasies make it more endearing.

Maybe your preoccupation with your body image is a way of not facing up to real difficulties.

Change your thinking from, "When I've lost some weight, I'll be happy," to "I'm happy; I want to look after my body."

"Enjoy your body . . . It's the greatest instrument you'll ever own."—Mary Schmich

Keep your body healthy and clean and dressed in great clothes because you are happy to be alive, but leave judgments about how your body looks to others. The pleasure, or displeasure, they get from looking at you comes from their preconceived notions of beauty.

What state does your body feel best in? Revved up and energetic, or calm and unhassled? Throughout the day, make a conscious effort to regain your optimal state.

50. creative
being artistic

"Everyone has talent. What is rare is the courage to follow the talent to the dark place where it leads."
—Erica Jong

Art is often used as a therapeutic tool, because when we express ourselves we can bypass our conscious mind and connect directly with the subconscious where our deepest fears and hurts are buried. Use art to find out who you are: Paint a dream; write the story of your family; sculpt your own body.

Keep track of the creative process by making it tangible. Tack interesting visuals to a wall; plaster a notice board with ideas. Chefs do this by taping up snapshots of finished dishes in their kitchens; stylists by gathering little collections of fabric swatches, buttons, and color chips. It's a way of making inspiration concrete.

You get more creative as you start to be more creative and think of yourself as being a more creative person. It's like a muscle that grows as you use it.

Creativity doesn't thrive in a judgmental environment. You have to feel safe to be able to experiment, play, make a fool of yourself.

There are two basic stages to the creative process: **input** and **incubation**. Input means collecting ideas, researching options, and getting excited about all the possibilities. You do it by looking outside yourself for fresh stimuli and saturating yourself in information that jump-starts your creative thinking. Look through obscure foreign magazines. Surf the Internet. Talk to people. Keep files of things that interest you. Fill your mind with every aspect of the problem you've set yourself and save all your ideas. (That's why creative people carry notebooks and sketchpads everywhere and jot things down on napkins.)

The second stage, incubation, is when your unconscious reorganizes and elaborates on the collected material. For it to do this, you need to switch off for a while, give up actively thinking, and just let solutions and creativity happen. Ideas will come when your body is relaxed and in a receptive frame of mind, when you are doing something you don't have to concentrate on too much, like swimming laps or driving.

To be more creative, spend time with creative people.

Define your problem. To have a brilliant idea, first you have to have a problem that the idea solves, whether it's how to represent a three-dimensional object in two dimensions, or what to have for dinner.

"Art is a lie that makes us realize the truth." —Picasso

You can think of winter as dead batteries, messy sidewalks, colds, flu, and misery, or as a chance to ski, make snowmen, and snuggle up to loved ones.

"In the midst of winter, I have finally discovered that there is within me an inevitable summer."

—Albert Camus

Winter blues? It might be SAD (Seasonal Affective Disorder), a kind of depression that comes during months of little sun. Our bodies need about ten times the amount of light that illuminates the average office. Try to get outside for a few minutes of sunshine a day.

Hot water is one of the most underappreciated luxuries in life. Rinse a washcloth in hot water, wring it out, then bury your face in the soothing warmth. Bliss after a long, busy day.

A doctor's tip for staying flu-free: Make it a habit to wash your hands as soon as you come home.

How to put up with winter: Take classes to create a new you by spring. Call another time zone and tell them it's the worst blizzard in living memory. Get chronic cabin fever: Refluff your comforter; invest in real sheepskin slippers; wear cashmere; order in; spend hours staring into a fire; whoosh down carpeted stairs on a teatray sled; host your own Monty Python festival. Embrace snow days as a chance to spend long afternoons with books, baking bread, knitting.

51. chilled

warming up winter

How to resist winter to the utmost: Visit a greenhouse and smell things growing; rent tropical movies; turn the central heating way up; read Caribbean travel brochures; spritz coconut suntan spray on your wrists; force freesia and narcissus bulbs; make your rooms brighter by cleaning the windows inside and out; fix frozen margaritas.

How to embrace the cold: Obsess about the weather—sit glued to the weather on TV, become an expert on wind-chill, winter storm watches, blizzard conditions, and record lows. Research the definitive hot chocolate recipe. Rejoice in the ability to forget about painting your toenails, or smoothing your legs, or getting a tan, and the fact that your extra five pounds is covered by sweaters. Simmer apple cider, cloves, and cinnamon together to make the house smell cozy. Outside, appreciate the new quiet, soft, white world; the look of trees iced in snow after a snowstorm; putting the first footprints on newly fallen snow; icicles; the bracing sting of bitter cold.

If you want to understand someone else more fully, try the "empty chair" technique from Gestalt therapy. Sit on one chair and place another empty chair facing you—imagine that the person you want to connect with is sitting on it. Describe to her exactly how you feel. Now, swap chairs and imagine yourself as the other person replying to you. How would she answer? What does she really want to say to you? Continue the conversation as long as it takes to understand someone else.

Sympathy is an emotional sharing of what someone is experiencing. If you get depressed when you are with someone who is depressed, that's sympathy. Empathy is when you understand someone's feelings but can stay objective enough to avoid becoming overwhelmed by those feelings. Empathetic people find some truth in what another is saying, even if they are convinced it is totally wrong, unreasonable, irrational, or unfair. They can see the world through someone else's frame of reference.

You can gain empathy by paraphrasing another person's words or by asking a question to see if you are reading his or her emotions correctly. Acknowledge a person's feelings and he will feel your empathy.

Pay less attention to what someone else does and more to how you respond. (Ask, "Why does it always make me crazy when he does this?" rather than trying to make him stop.) The only person you have control over is yourself.

52. empathetic

If someone says, "Sometimes life seems meaningless," it is not empathetic to reply in a way that stops all discussion (to say, for example, "Nonsense, cheer up"). It's better to say something like "You must be feeling really low to believe that." This answer shows that you accept the other's feelings but don't necessarily agree with them, and makes it easier for the other person to reveal what's worrying her.

To gain more empathy for a person, simply think about her often—keep her in mind, wonder how she is getting on.

The face of the enemy frightens me only when I see how much it resembles mine."
—Stanislaw Jerzy Lec

If you lack close, caring relationships, try to connect with anyone and everyone you meet during the day. Commiserate with others waiting in line; ask the bus driver how his day's going; smile at children.

Treasure those people with whom you can most easily be yourself.

53. Indecisive

making decisions

Visualize yourself living each choice. How do you feel? What is your gut reaction? Listen to your body. If it sends signals of physical or emotional distress, pay attention.

"In the small matters trust the mind, in the large ones the heart."
—Sigmund Freud

To make a decision less threatening, and to clarify your feelings, try explaining the situation to someone who doesn't know anything about it, even if this conversation is held only in your mind. Other ways to gain perspective: Describe the problem to yourself as if it were happening to someone else, or write a letter as if you were asking Dear Abby what to do. You'll gain insight from trying to frame the problem in words.

Think about all your options before you evaluate them. Are you restricting yourself unnecessarily? Maybe you shouldn't be agonizing whether to do A, but choosing among A, B, C, or D.

There is no "right" decision. There are just choices and consequences. It's up to you to make those consequences ones you want to live with.

If you have been gnawing at a problem for weeks, maybe it's time to take a break and let your subconscious work on it for a while. Mark a date on your calendar by which to make a final decision and try to distract yourself until then. Take the pressure off and the answer will come.

What will happen if you don't make any decision at all?

Sometimes pro and con lists help; sometimes they seem much too simplistic. Instead, try keeping a journal. Over a week or so, write down what friends recommend, your own changing thoughts on the subject, and lists of the compromises that each option would necessitate. Make a tally of best-case results and worst-case results. Frame the problem in as many different ways as possible: not just "Should we get divorced?" but "Would it be better to live alone?" Don't think in terms of simply for and against, but what would give you the most satisfaction. Match your options against your priorities, try to find an answer for each of the objections you raise to yourself. Reading these notes back, even after only a few days, gives you a bigger picture.

Give yourself all the facts and information you need to make a decision. Do your research, find out how long you'd have to commit for, and test each alternative as much as you can before you decide.

54. blocked
brainstorming solutions

■ Brainstorming is a good way to come up with a whole lot of ideas fast. Originally it was a group-think exercise, but one person with a pencil and paper can effectively brainstorm alone, by following these rules:

1. Form your problem into a question, or do a little sketch or diagram of it.
2. As fast as you can, write down every single idea that comes to you, no matter how ridiculous, impossible, or impractical it may be. Use a stack of index cards, taking one card per idea. Ideally, each thought will lead to another and another—try to expand on the last. Move in any direction you want. Go for zany, farfetched, crazy ideas. Aim for quantity, not quality, and keep going as long as you can.
3. Don't edit yet. Don't judge or evaluate or criticize anything you come up with. Make sure every thought is legible and coherent; then put the notes away until later. When you look through them again, more ideas may come.

Throughout the day, ask anyone you encounter—the doorman, your five-year-old—for their ideas and suggestions. They may not seem relevant, but could lead to something useful when combined or compared with your own ideas.

■ **When evaluating, see if the drawbacks of the best idea can be solved by one of the others. Can any idea be modified, rearranged, reversed, magnified, or paired with another?**

■ Lateral thinking is another way to generate lots of ideas. Use a random stimulus, which could be a list of simple, familiar words, such as those found in a child's dictionary. Juxtapose each word in turn with the problem. Your mind will attempt to develop a pathway from the word to the problem—and change your view of it.

■ Mindmapping is a more graphic variation of brainstorming: Write, draw, or diagram your problem in the middle of a large piece of paper and enclose it in a circle. Free-associate by drawing lines radiating from the circle, like the spokes of a wheel, and at the end of each write the first word that comes to mind. When you've come up with as many associations as you can from the first word, draw lines radiating out from the new words and list your associations from them, too, until the paper is covered with a network of interlocking thoughts. When you are finished, underline words that recur and connect related themes.

55. drowsy ZZZZZZZZZZZZZ

staying awake

Here is a series of actions to wake you up when your energy is flagging. Do each step, or find a similar alternative.

1. Run cold water over your wrists or splash cold water on your face.
2. Brush your hair, preferably with one of those scalp-massaging brushes with little rubber nodules on the end of each bristle.
3. Suck a peppermint, as much for the smell as the taste. Or peel open an orange and sniff. Any citrus rind will give you a lift. Or splash on a revitalizing cologne—jasmine is a picker-upper.
4. Bend over and touch your toes to rev up circulation—or go for a walk around the block to get some sun and fresh air.
5. Look at something brightly colored to perk up your brain. (A good excuse to buy flowers for your desk, or a painting for the wall.)
6. Breathe deeply.

After a big meal, the blood flow to the brain decreases and goes instead to your stomach to aid digestion. So if you need to stay awake, avoid early afternoon slump by eating a small lunch.

Sometimes a nap will get you through the day after a night of little sleep. Drink a cup of coffee just before settling down—by the time the caffeine kicks in twenty minutes later, you've had the ideal length nap. Sleep too much longer and you'll drift into deep sleep mode and wake up groggy.

Wake yourself up by stimulating all the senses: Get out into the sun; smell the coffee; turn on toe-tapping music; use tingly shower gel; and, if you can bear it, alternate the water temperature from hot to cold.

When you recognize, accept, and express all of who you are, you have access to more energy.

A cup of tea is both stimulating and calming at the same time.

For energy, snack on a mixture of protein and carbohydrates like yogurt and cereal, peanut butter and crackers, or hummus and pita bread.

Don't underestimate how your thoughts and feelings can give you energy. After a tiring day, you may not be able to get yourself interested in cleaning out a closet, but if a friend came up with tickets to something you wanted to see, you'd have a renewed burst of vitality.

Rub your palms together briskly for few seconds, until they are warm, then cup them over your closed eyes to revitalize them.

If your life were a movie, what point are you up to in the plot? What would be the next scene?

If you keep going the way you're going, will you be happy five years from now, to have done what you've chosen by default?

What do you want to experience? Have you ever taken a hot-air balloon ride, lived on an island, watched a baby being born?

change

Growth happens from the inside out. Don't just react to life; make good things happen. When you take steps toward where you want to go, all sorts of things open up. What's stopping you from getting what you want out of life? Are there concrete, practical obstacles in your way, or are you sabotaging yourself? When we feel secure, we take risks. When we're under pressure, we go back to old ways of behaving.

Make a tiny life change to point you in a new direction. Start small: Wake up an hour earlier; decide to accept every invitation that comes your way next month; try sleeping with your head where your feet usually go; order something on the menu that you've never tried before.

experience

56. apathetic

getting out of a rut

"I keep forgetting.
Am I in the groove,
or in a rut?"

—Mal Hancock

Attempt something you're not quite sure you can pull off. Go out on a limb—that's where the sweetest fruit is.

"If you want to live more than one life you've got to die more than once."

—Françoise Giroud

If you need too much control over the outcome of a venture, if you always have to know exactly what the day will bring, if you worry what people think, you're not living life to the fullest. What do you need to feel fully alive right now?

Like a baby who lets go of his beloved stuffed bunny to grab at a cookie, growth means reaching out to new experiences, and in the process, letting go of old ones.

You're never too old to be bold.

"Don't worry about what the world wants of you, worry about what makes you come alive."

—Lawrence LeShan

A bird in a cage forgets how to sing. What are you trying to protect yourself from? Is there something insurmountable that's holding you back, or is it your thinking? Avoiding risks limits personal growth. You don't have to wait for permission from anyone to start living fully.

growth

What do you no longer have time for? What do you want to achieve while there's still time? The older you get, the less energy you should waste at a job you hate, or being with people or events that don't interest you.

Life can be divided into two phases: The first half you look outward, learn skills, gain knowledge, and do things. The second half you look inward, reflect on the meaning of life; *be* rather than do. The good news is that the first half provides you with what you need to make the most of the second half. You become whole. You get more control of your life and self. You appreciate relationships and rediscover nature and things of the spirit. You become all too aware that you are mortal—but this makes you value more the time you have.

"It's never too late to be what you might have been."

—George Eliot

The only way to ensure sufficient fuss is made of your birthday is to plan it yourself.

No matter how old you are now, in five years you will be five years older, no matter whether you spent those years getting a degree or having your teeth straightened or doing whatever else you thought you were too old to attempt.

You are emotionally mature when the three parts of your personality—childish desire, responsible adult, and guiding conscience—all work well together; when you are enthusiastic about life, able to form adult emotional relationships, able to express anger when necessary, able to make independent decisions, and able to face adversity without loss of faith in yourself.

57. Antiquated

feeling old

When you are in your twenties, you're obsessed with what people think about you. When you are fifty, you realize that, in fact, nobody was thinking about you; they were too busy worrying about what you thought of them.

The older you get, the fewer people there are to push you around.

What would you like to know in ten years' time that you don't know now? What can you do now so that you'll look back happily then?

Think about the twelve-year-old you—if you could talk to her now, what would she say? What would she think of you?

What do you fear when you get scared at the thought of getting old? How can you prevent those fears from coming true?

58. Confidence
positive speaking

Your mind retains images more clearly than words. So if you imagine hearing a positive statement as if someone else were actually speaking the words, those words will become more meaningful to you.

There are two reasons to talk to yourself in a positive way. First, it's difficult to work toward a goal that is stated negatively—that's like making a shopping list of all things you don't need to buy. Second, when you dwell on negative things you draw them to you—when your horoscope says you'll be unlucky, you start looking for unlucky experiences.

Make an affirmation plausible and realistic. If you keep repeating "I feel fantastic" when you don't, your mind won't accept the idea and the exercise will seem ridiculous. Don't deny the negative, but find a phrase that offers hope.

If you tell yourself, "Don't forget the milk," you are much more likely to forget it than if you framed the phrase as "Remember the milk." The key words of the first are *forget milk*, the key words of the second are *remember milk*—the complete opposite. Focusing on the positive is much more likely to achieve a positive outcome. Similarly, you'll give a more reliable impression if you use helpful phrases like "certainly" and "sure" in everyday speech, rather than phrases that include negative words, such as "No problem."

Many self-help books recognize the power of positive statements, or affirmations. We all talk to ourselves—affirmations are a way of being aware that we're giving ourselves good messages rather than self-defeating ones. Affirmations will make you feel better about yourself, but only if you frame them properly. They should be statements that start with the word "I," and they should be positively rather than negatively phrased and in the present tense. Don't adopt an affirmation you've read in a book; instead, compose one that is meaningful to you. Use an image or metaphor—a house being built, a caterpillar metamorphosing into a butterfly—if that helps.

"You have to name it to claim it."
—Phillip C. McGraw,
Life Strategies

To find out more about how our minds respond and react to language, investigate neurolinguistic programming (NLP).

Repeat a positive statement throughout the day. Make it into a screensaver on your computer, or tape it to your bathroom mirror. If you hear or see a phrase enough times, it stays in your subconscious—that's what makes advertisements and radio jingles so effective.

59. TENSE

TAKING TIME OUT

Our mind works with pictures more instinctively than it does with words, and our body responds to images more directly. If you say to yourself "relax," you are not likely to. More effective is to imagine being in a relaxing place. Athletes know the value of this—before muscles act, they are prompted by thoughts.

When the present is too much, leave your surroundings; take a few moments to dream or visualize something wonderful.

"It's not that I'm out of touch with reality. It's just that I have a bad opinion of it."
—G. P. Greenwood

When you imagine a soothing place, you can develop your own Pavlovian response, a shortcut to relaxation. Every time you visualize your peaceful place, put your hand on your heart or link the thought to some other physical cue. Eventually just putting your hand on your heart will bring peace and relaxation. In fact, you can call up any emotion you want whenever you want, if you take the time to make the association between the feeling and the trigger. To get in the habit of feeling more confident, for example, twist the ring on your finger as you recall times in your life when you have been supremely confident. Do this so many times that eventually, whenever you want to feel confident, all you have to do is twist your ring.

Create peace by sending your mind on a minivacation. Sort through your memories until you recall a time and place where you felt absolutely at peace. Visualize a view you love, or any place where you have been happy and relaxed. The more detail you can conjure up, the better you can visualize and think yourself right there, the more completely you'll re-create that inner harmony and the calmer you will become. Relive the experience as fully as you can, using all your senses. Begin by thinking about what you see, the blue of the water, the far-off misty hills. Then listen for the slap of the waves against the boat or the sound of birds. Smell the ocean or the pine trees, feel the sun and the sea spray on your face. If one memory doesn't work, search for another—a pleasant, satisfying place to go that consistently conjures up peace for you. Do it wholeheartedly and you'll be able to take refreshing little five-minute vacations whenever you need to.

Change your **perspective:**
Slow down; lie down on the floor.
Watch the clouds or the stars in the infinite night sky.

Touch life. Embrace your friends; stroke your dog or cat.

la la la

Sing

It is hard to worry and sing at the same time.

Hug yourself safe: Wrap your arms around yourself, picture yourself at five years old and imagine that your arms are around that child, holding her close. Then imagine that you're the five-year-old child and that your arms are around the waist of the person who's soothing you.

How to get time alone when the house is full of people:
Take a whole afternoon to get your hair highlighted and your nails done • Attend a church service or exercise class alone • Send your mind on a brief vacation: Do some gardening; lose yourself in a murder mystery or a favorite concerto • Become a member of a museum and go there to sit and read or write in a favorite room or eat at the coffee shop • Tell everyone you're going to be a half-hour late because you're stuck in traffic; then go to an art gallery, greenhouse, or library to find a different atmosphere, or browse in your favorite store.

60. overwhelmed

instant fixes

Stress becomes overwhelming when you start to feel that everything is spinning out of control. To get a grip, find something about the situation you can regain power over or direct. Even a small change helps: Find a more comfortable chair, take off clothes that bind, put on some soothing music, make a list.

Massage relaxes muscles, increases circulation, rubs out body stress. Do it for yourself: Massage your feet; massage one shoulder at a time; put both hands at the base of the back of your neck and knead the tight muscles there. There's usually a lot of tension in the jaw when we're stressed, too. Find a way of relieving that muscle tension—groan or yawn or stretch. Or screw up your face as tight as you can, and then open your mouth and eyes wide.

There is great comfort in being a good mother to yourself. Give yourself reassurance and a sense of being cherished; treat yourself as you wish you were treated as a child, or with the care and love you provide your own children. Would you allow your kids to eat what you ate today? Would you allow them to feel bad and not get any help?

If you are visiting a child in the hospital, good toys to take are ones that help him or her communicate with others, like hand puppets or magic tricks. Or take an autograph book or blackboard where visitors can write funny messages; or take simple crafts to become involved in, such as origami papers. Hanging mobiles, wind chimes, or prisms provide something to watch.

Ideally, an act of kindness opens the lines of communication with others, giving you a feeling of being part of a nurturing community and the world—and this connection makes you feel more in tune with who you are. One of the first lessons we learn as babies is that we can't get by alone. We've evolved to have feelings of love, empathy, guilt, and pity to bind us to our fellow humans—whom we need for our own survival and emotional well-being.

Be the kind of person you would want to have as a friend. Overlook minor insults and criticisms.

Do what you like doing anyway, but do it for a good cause. Knit sweaters for oil-spill-affected penguins, adopt a child, volunteer to shop for someone.

Try to make real your highest aspirations, not for anyone else, but because it will make you feel good.

61. altruistic
volunteering

A good way of working through your own crisis or life problem is to work for a worthy cause related to it. When you actively right a wrong, or support the similarly afflicted, you help both yourself and the cause.

Volunteering shouldn't mean sacrificing your own happiness for someone else's. Pitch in for the "helper's high" you get when you give of yourself. Start small. Begin with little doses of altruism, like helping a mother with a baby carriage up the escalator, or holding open doors. You don't have to change the world on a grand scale, but you can make it a better place, one good deed at a time.

"We make a living by what we get, but we make a life by what we give."

—Winston Churchill

Social support, giving it and getting it, is the mortar that binds the world.

Ways to make a difference: Befriend an elderly neighbor, volunteer at your favorite charity or organization whose goals you feel in tune with, join or start a pressure group, plant native plants or bulbs or trees wherever you can, teach first aid, teach adults to read and write.

62. Empty?
who are you

"How many cares one loses when one decides not to be something, but to be someone."
—Coco Chanel

Do you find yourself spending time you don't have, doing things you don't enjoy, to impress people you don't particularly like? Becoming aligned with your purpose in life makes it more satisfying and meaningful. To be happy, you need something to be enthusiastic about.

If you were a company, what would your mission statement be? A mission statement is a unifying and motivating sentence or paragraph that focuses on what an organization wants to accomplish. Most mission statements have two parts—the concrete and the ideal—to make a product and to do it well. A personal mission statement is a way of crystallizing your vision for yourself, working out what's important to you, deciding where you want to go and the principles on which these achievements will be based. One person's mission statement might be: To express myself through writing in a way that helps people. To find yours, think of what you are doing when you're fulfilled and happy, and ask yourself why you do it.

When you have a vision of yourself, you can align your goals and work to make them a reality. Don't just think "I'd like to be a teacher," think of yourself as a teacher, and work from there. The outer realities will then align themselves in the same way iron filings align themselves in the presence of a magnetic field.

Start saying out loud, "I want . . . I want . . ." and adding whatever comes to mind, for as long as you can. Let whatever floats up from your unconscious be examined.

What good characteristics do your loved ones see in you? Can you see those qualities in yourself?

What would the title of your autobiography be? If your life philosophy could be summarized on a T-shirt, what would it be?

Fulfillment comes from having a sense of your own worth, knowing what makes you happy, balancing the responsibilities in your life, and finding your place in the community.

What represents success to you? Even more important, how will you know when you get it? In what way will you feel differently from how you are feeling right now?

What do you want out of life? Describe what it is as if to a very young child.

63. cluttered

spring-clean your life

Lighten up! When you have little that pins you down you can travel to new places, have adventures on a whim, quit worrying about burglars and insurance.

To feel clean and new, toss stuff out. To motivate yourself, ask these questions of each item:

- What does this help me accomplish? Nothing? Throw it away.
- How easy would it be to replace this? Can it be replaced for under $10?
- Could someone else use and enjoy this?
- If I ever take up again the activity that these tools are used for, won't I want more up-to-date tools?
- Interview each object. Ask it how it is helping you and where it belongs in your life.
- Edit. Save only the best of your collections.

Ask yourself what would happen if you didn't bother doing the things that don't make you happy. If you don't love doing it and don't have to do it—don't do it!

Plant a seed this spring: Work toward a single summer goal.

> Don't hold on to ghosts. If an object that belonged to your parents or your childhood is weighing you down, take a photo of it (or commemorate it in some other way), and then let it go.

For a new start, shed old skins like a snake. Discard long hair, your stilettos, your preconceptions. Toss out your old, restrictive definitions of anything: balanced meals, what you should be doing, the right way to do things.

Don't keep anything that's not beautiful, useful, or loved.

If you're someone with a strong inner taskmaster, start following your own whims, especially when there's no reason not to do so. Want to walk back a block and check out a shoe store when you're in no pressing hurry? Do it. You'll be surprised how your satisfaction with life rises when you regularly indulge yourself like this.

Toss out the old; take the chance you'll find better.

Instead of taking a vacation to somewhere, take a vacation from something.

Make a spring ritual of trying something you've never done before: landscape architecture, t'ai chi, growing African violets.

Spring-clean yourself: Toss out critical thoughts along with the brown blusher. Decide to carry a backpack instead of a purse, to use a kind word rather than a critical one. Refresh your outlook; update your dreams. Eliminate what you're not and what's left will be you.

64. Amused

laughing more

Get more laughter into your life: Keep books and videos on hand that make you giggle out loud. Assemble a folder filled with funny clippings and cartoons today—don't wait until you are feeling blue; you won't be motivated then.

Why did laughter evolve? Researchers believe it plays a part in social bonding, solidifying friendships, and pulling people into a group. Smiles are our first form of communication with another person—as a baby, and with strangers.

Play peek-a-boo with a baby. Get a puppy. Hang around with funny people. Rediscover the old silent movies. Try to see the world through the eyes of your favorite comic.

When you laugh, you become more relaxed. Even anticipating a funny event lowers stress. Laughter relieves an accumulation of nervous energy—think of it as a massage from the inside out.

It's been said that blood pressure, heart rate, muscle tension, and stress hormone levels all drop when you laugh. Opinion is divided over whether laughter really does promote physical healing. Perhaps it isn't so much laughing that heals but the beneficial effect of humor when used to confront life's challenges.

Laughing is a physical reflex, an automatic, convulsive spasm of the respiratory mechanism that occurs when we realize that there is more than one way to interpret the stimuli we are experiencing. We also laugh when we feel two contradictory emotions or when two frameworks of reference that normally are separate are brought together in a way that seems to connect them. It's a startled response of the brain. We laugh when we're relieved and surprised, or when the unexpected happens.

Teachers know that laughter helps keep students interested. It makes us more receptive to new experiences, creates emotional intimacy, and encourages us to take ourselves less seriously.

Like yawning, laughter is contagious. You'll laugh more if you are with large groups of people who are in a mood to laugh, and if you are in a relaxed setting and feeling uninhibited. We laugh most often not in response to jokes, but when we're in happy relationships with friends.

Humor is one of the best and most psychologically mature and healthy defenses. (In other words, it's a good way of controlling negative emotions.) Even when in great emotional pain, humor helps you detach from an event and maintain your dignity and a sense of self. When you make jokes about a bad situation, you still feel the bad feelings, but you can control them better.

65. **Worried**
good worry vs. bad worry

Worry is good when it prepares you for the future—when you anticipate problems and figure out solutions to them and think about the consequences of your actions. Turn paralyzing, obsessive worry into good worry: Instead of thinking, "What if that happened?" think, "What would I do if that happened?" Constructive planning feels good; worry doesn't.

It's important to understand that crises and problems don't make you worry—worry is something you do to yourself. And negative thoughts are a dangerous bad habit because by repeating something over and over you make it true—it's called self-hypnosis!

Worry becomes negative when it is repetitive, unproductive, unnecessary. You need to shake off this kind of worry forcefully by consciously changing your thinking. Don't let your mind settle into a routine of negativity; don't let worry become an end in itself.

If your active imagination makes pictures of your worries, use your imagination to shrink the picture smaller and smaller until it disappears.

Make a list of your problems; then decide which of these four categories each worry falls into:

- important and controllable
- important and uncontrollable
- unimportant and controllable
- unimportant and uncontrollable

You can do something about circumstances if you can control them; if not, it's no use worrying.

What's the cause of your obsessive, chronic worry? Might it be an excuse for avoiding real problems? Or is it a comfortingly familiar habit that makes you feel you're in control? Perhaps you've inherited constant anxiety from a mother who believed that a good mom is one who never stops worrying.

Pain is what you feel; suffering is what you tell yourself you feel.

Suffering is optional.

Have short, regular worry sessions when all you do is worry—your quota for the day. Set a timer for ten minutes, and go somewhere out of the way, so you won't associate worry with your daily environment. Then, worry constructively: Get the facts, think of every possible outcome, make a plan, write out steps to take. Don't waste this time blaming yourself—you'll accomplish more if you are on your own side. Once the worry session is over, deflect your thoughts when they try to return to your problems.

What's the absolute worst that can happen? Is there really something to fear? What do I accomplish by this worry? How will I feel about this a year from now?

66. isolated

creating family

Create your own "family" by spending more time with kindred spirits, people who make you feel happy, alive, and comfortable. Find your "tribe," people who have outlooks similar to yours, and who are at a similar life stage. A family of choice can help you feel less isolated and pressured and be a source of strength and encouragement far beyond your real family.

If you get no happiness from relationships, think about your relationship with your parents when you were a young child. If they were too intrusive, you may fear being "engulfed" by those whom you attempt to get close to. We gravitate to partners whose personalities remind us of our parents—we seek out behavior we expect.

"The answer doesn't lie in learning how to protect yourself from life. It lies in learning how to strengthen yourself so you can let a bit more of it in."
—Mildred Newman, Bernard Berkowitz, How to Be Your Own Best Friend: A Conversation with Two Psychoanalysts

Do you feel threatened by intimacy with others? Do you choose isolation as easier to bear?

Human beings are highly social, communal animals, evolved to live in families and communities. We become depressed and eccentric when we don't connect with others regularly. With strong social support, we get less stressed. No matter how much you value your independence, you need others for your well-being and happiness. You need a feeling of being a part of something larger than yourself. This needing of other people can scare some loners; they defend themselves by disparagement, indifference, and contempt. A healthy person recognizes his own unique personality but also his connection with others.

> "When you're at home with yourself, you're comfortable with who you are."
> —Oprah Winfrey

Loners need to relax into themselves and to accept themselves for who and what they are so they can be comfortable with others.

How have you handled solitude so far in your life? Constructively or destructively?

There are good things about living alone—everything is always where you left it, you can play a song over and over—but too much loneliness and isolation (solitary confinement) can give even strong people distorted perceptions and cause hallucinations and negative thoughts. If you're not married and don't have friends, try to connect in other relationships, and in as many ways as you can. Reach out to neighbors and colleagues where you work or play or learn; feel part of an institution or organization.

Tell someone as straightforwardly as possible how you feel wronged. Relate in objective, brief, neutral, nonblaming terms the behavior you don't like; explain what effect it has on your feelings; and explain the tangible effect the behavior has on your life. You might say, for example: "When you are late, I feel annoyed, because I waste time."

An important part of being assertive is having an aura of assertiveness. Look strong, confident, and self-assured through your body language.

When someone "won't take no for an answer," the best way to say no is to use the Broken Record technique: Repeat what you want calmly but with mechanical persistence. When doing this, it's important to always use the same phrase and to repeat it as many times as necessary. Don't get sidetracked or drawn into any other arguments, issues, or responses. If the other person responds with silence, wait until he or she fills it. Use this technique when making a justified request or to retain emotional control when you want a quick response and not an argument. It's particularly useful when saying no to high-pressure salespeople, but it's not an appropriate way to resolve problems with people close to you.

Don't use submissive phrases such as "I don't suppose you would—" or aggressive phrases such as "You'd better—." Instead, use direct, honest, assertive phrases that are firm about your needs, such as: "I'm not comfortable with that. What I'd prefer would be—."

67. ineffectual
becoming ASSERTIVE

Aggressive people insist on getting their own way. Passive people repress their own needs in order to please others. Assertive people demonstrate that they respect their own rights and those of others—but insist on being heard. The extent to which you can assert yourself is a measure of your self-esteem.

Rather than be aggressive or submit to disrupting behavior, give a choice instead of an ultimatum. You might, for example, let noisy kids decide between playing outside or being quiet in the house.

Our natural instinct is to cope with invasion or danger by choosing flight or fight. Assertive behavior is the healthy midpoint between the two, possible because humans can speak and solve problems. This doesn't mean that you should always be assertive, but try to avoid the subversive, controlling methods of interacting (guilt, whining) that the submissive person uses, or the alienating, dehumanizing methods the aggressive person uses.

Live in the present—
it's the only moment you have.
Use all your senses to enjoy right now, the way children and dogs do. It's about letting go and relaxing, being absorbed in what you're doing, savoring the moment. Joy comes from paying attention to all the little, gentle pleasures of an ordinary day—the feel of the sun in early spring, a phone call from a friend, a cup of coffee. Resolve to derive every bit of enjoyment from whatever comes your way.

> ". . . [Y]ou feel real joy in direct proportion to how connected you are to living your truth."
> —Oprah Winfrey

> You have lots of reasons to be happy. You also have lots of reasons to be unhappy. Happiness is a matter of choosing which to be.

It seems as if moods are a reaction to some event.
You spilled the sugar, say, and feel annoyed—but it's usually the other way around. You may have spilled the sugar because you were annoyed about something that your mind was mulling over as you reached for the sugar bowl. If you are in a joyful mood, you'll just say, "Oops!" and clean it up. If you are in a bad mood, you'll curse yourself. In other words, the spilled sugar doesn't cause the mood; rather, the mood dictates how you'll react to the incident.

68. *Joyful*

feeling happy

Human beings have long tried to understand what makes some people happier than others. In the Middle Ages, people believed that excess fluids in the body governed moods and actions. The ideal was to have the four "humors" in perfect balance. These days we know that, in fact, an imbalance of hormones can affect moods and influence day-to-day changes in our behavior. The two brain chemicals serotonin and norepinephrine seem to be natural antidepressants—and the body makes these from the foods we eat. So a well-balanced diet is important—not just for a healthy body, but to stay as happy as possible, too.

> Joy is not a trivial diversion; it's vital. If something brings you joy, it should have an important place in your life.

When you feel joy, savor the good feeling. Recognize the joy, and what led to it.

Try to avoid those people who constantly complain, condemn your joys and dreams, and are always whining. These people can drain the happiness out of any atmosphere.

What you think about all day long determines the moods you have and how you feel. You can't stop thoughts from popping into your mind, but you can decide not to dwell on negative thoughts.

Think of your mood as a psychological thermometer. Tune into how you are feeling during the day. Express these emotions to yourself and, when that becomes a habit, to other people.

Mood researcher Dr. Robert Thayer theorizes that our levels of energy and anxiety fluctuate during the day, and that in different combinations they create what we call moods. When we have high energy and low tension, we're in a state of "calm energy" (a good mood); high energy, high tension is an agitated "tense-energy" mood. When we're tired and tense ("tense-tired"), we're in a bad mood. A low-energy, low-tension state ("calm-tiredness") is a subdued, passive mood. Thayer says we subconsciously try to regulate our moods throughout the day; by, for example, drinking a cup of coffee in an attempt to move from a calm-tired mood to a calm-energy mood.

"Our life is what our thoughts make it." —Marcus Aurelius

To learn more about your thoughts and how you can choose not to act on negative ones, read about cognitive behavioral therapy and the theories of Aaron T. Beck, M.D.

69. moody
controlling your emotions

Remember the last time a friend was late and how you worried that she'd had an accident? Thinking about a friend being in danger puts you in an anxious mood. That mood changes to anger when you see your friend and realize she didn't bother calling to tell you she would be late. Your thoughts about the incident have changed, even though nothing has changed in the real world.

The psychologist Hans Eysenck classified personality by arranging moods in a circular spectrum, with *stable, introverted, unstable,* and *extroverted* being the four points of the compass. An agitated, overexcited mood is the other extreme from a calm, despondent mood. Extroverted, outward-directed behavior is opposite from introverted, inward-directed behavior. Throughout our lives, most of us tend to stay in one area. You can become more balanced if you try to move yourself more toward the opposite side of the compass from where you are now. Happiness is equilibrium.

When you understand how your thoughts create your moods, you can separate yourself from them so they won't influence your feelings. Pay attention to your mood changes and the thinking that brought them about. Try to catch yourself just as a negative thought arises. Tell yourself, "I'm having angry thoughts," and then decide how to deal with them.

Fear of failure happens when you have made what you are doing the one and only avenue of achieving recognition. It's maintaining the illusion that some day you might achieve something worthwhile instead of risking the hurt that would come with rejection.

Overcome the fear of doing something poorly by consciously doing what you're afraid of. Purposely write a terrible poem, make a fool of yourself, paint an ugly picture. You may find that you produce your best work! But if it is bad, so what? Be aware of how you felt when you purposely tried to fail. What does it say about you if you do things badly? Why does that matter?

Freewriting is a good way to loosen up and work out what's bothering you, no matter what type of work you're trying to do. This is a way of catching the unconscious off guard and allowing it to break through. Take paper and pen, set yourself a topic (the emotion or mood you are in right now, for example), and start writing whatever comes to mind. Don't bother with punctuation or grammar, or even whether you are making sense, just keep going—write without stopping. If you can't think about what to say, write about that, but keep the pen moving. This is free association, allowing the mind to wander freely and explore thoughts without censorship. Don't read what you've written until you stop. The aim of this stream-of-consciousness writing is not to increase your skills as a writer but to tap into creativity.

70. **stymied** breaking through

Instead of pushing yourself to complete work that's not going well, see if a change helps. Write the report in a coffee shop instead of at your desk, or move to a different part of the project for a few hours. Try changing the way you measure the amount you've achieved: do two hours' worth rather than two pages' worth. Or change your medium: Use a tape recorder instead of a legal pad; a paintbrush rather than a roller; index cards rather than a computer.

You can't be creative if you are concerned about other people's opinions, or when trying to protect yourself from criticism. The less you look to others for applause, the more freedom and confidence you start to feel.

Fear of failure is a fear of being judged—and the ways in which you fear you'll be judged are directly related to your own self-doubts.

71. pessimistic

faulty thinking

To flush out your bad thinking habits, brag about yourself. Immediately, a cynical little voice in your head will dispute those claims. Say "I'm terrific," and hear, "Yeah, right." Have a dialogue with that carping voice about the self-doubts that leap to mind.

Your thoughts create your emotions. To test this, try feeling an emotion without first thinking about something that inspires the emotion—it's not possible. To control your pessimism, understand that your thoughts are just thoughts, not reality.

Do you always expect a negative outcome to every situation? Do you judge and condemn everyone you come in contact with? Do people say you have a "chip on your shoulder"? Criticism is such an unproductive way of trying to change anything, including yourself. Animals and children, for example, change their behavior most effectively when they're rewarded for doing the right thing, not nagged about the bad.

We all have an "attributional style"—excuses we've (unconsciously) developed to explain the good and bad things that happen to us. For example, telling yourself "I always mess up," or "I can't do anything right," or "It's all my fault" is a way of not facing up to reality. There are several common kinds of pessimistic thinking patterns that are easy to fall into: deciding that a whole project is ruined if just one thing goes wrong; blowing negative events out of proportion; assuming your pessimistic feelings reflect the truth; or being convinced something is a fact even though you have no proof. These distorted thought patterns are bad habits. Discipline yourself to divert destructive thoughts as soon as you have them. If you were enjoying a tennis match, you would not let stray thoughts interrupt your concentration—it's possible to ignore any thought you want to ignore.

If your negative internal voices have a familiar personal refrain—you often deride your own looks or intelligence, for example—you are using yourself as a scapegoat for pain and anxiety. You're turning the hurt into a civil war. Instead, investigate the pain or anxiety. Ask yourself why you're eating an extra slice of pizza: Why do you feel the need to comfort yourself with it? Self-condemnation won't heal the pain.

When you tell yourself "I can't," do you mean you don't want to, or that you've decided not to? When you tell yourself "I should," do you mean you legally or morally should or just that you want to?

72. iNCompetent

boosting self-esteem

Psychologists have classified several different kinds of human intelligence: mathematical, spatial, verbal, musical, and emotional. There's also kinesthetic intelligence, which is the ability to perform skilled body movements or manipulate intricate objects. Instead of disparaging your own intellect, discover which area of intelligence you excel in.

It's up to you to give yourself recognition for all the things you've achieved. When you do something you are proud of—parked the car neatly, honored a commitment to yourself, diverted a negative thought—dwell on it for a few minutes. Praise yourself; savor the experience. Own your successes. It's important: It makes you feel good and it spurs you on to do better things.

Self-esteem is your decision to treat yourself as a beloved, worthy friend. That means respecting yourself, taking care of yourself, nurturing yourself. Self-esteem is the composite of all our feelings about who we are.

Self-esteem is confidence. Spend time doing something you are good at to remind yourself of your skills. And keep learning: master a new computer program, learn how to windsurf or how to whip up a great omelette. Nothing makes you feel better about yourself than a new accomplishment. And if you need encouragement, look at photos of yourself as a child. Think of all the things you can do now that you couldn't do then.

Many variables, such as the time of day, lack of sleep, or a change in hormone levels, affect your moods and color how you think about yourself. When you are feeling down, your self-confidence will be low. Know that this feeling is temporary and work harder to react positively to negative thoughts about yourself. Recall a time when you were confident, and remember those positive feelings. Recreate the posture, movement, and gestures that went with the feelings.

Another reason to exercise: When you get physically strong, you are much more confident in all areas of your life.

Self-esteem can quickly spiral downward: Having low self-confidence means that you will probably perform poorly, so you avoid the activity and feel bad about yourself, which leads to even lower self-confidence. Send the spiral back up by feeling good about yourself.

The foundations of your self-esteem were set at a very early age. If you were not made to feel loved, valued, important, significant, wanted, respected, trusted, and approved of by your parents, you must learn to feel this way about yourself.

73. misanthropic

coping with holidays

If your family places more importance on giving gifts than on doing things together, gifts will become a great burden. Aim to de-escalate a little every holiday season. For friends who insist on exchanging presents, buy simple little items in bulk to use as spur-of-the-moment gifts for everyone, rather than making yourself crazy trying to find something perfect for each person. Choose poinsettia plants or amaryllis, copies of Charles Dickens's *A Christmas Carol*, sprigs of mistletoe, nonperishable fancy foods, or handmade holiday ornaments.

The endless obligations, the regressive sibling rivalry, the crowded airports, the hollow season's "bleet-ings," the turkey torpor. No wonder you become a misanthropic Grinch when the season of "comfort and joy" isn't. But no one is forcing you to exhaust yourself. This year, resolve to partake only in the holiday activities that inspire you to feel goodwill toward everyone. You won't lose the holiday spirit, you'll find it.

If you can manage just one moment of feeling peace and goodwill to mankind per day during the holidays, that's enough.

Meaningful rituals give our lives predictability and stability, a sense of security and comfort. They make us happy in three ways: through anticipation, as we enjoy them, and by providing good memories. But it's important to retain only the traditions that you and your family really appreciate and to use them to reconnect with people you love. Keep rituals simple so nobody has too much to prepare.

Simplify: Forget the Victorian gingerbread house made from scratch, the handmade holly wreaths, the grape-studded cranberry gelatin ring that nobody eats. Instead, order in delicacies for a Christmas Eve supper that doesn't require cooking, use silver foil from the kitchen as gift wrap, make cutout reindeer masks, or white paper snowflake place mats with the kids.

The holiday misery you feel remains true to your childhood. But you'll never change your dysfunctional extended family; you can only change yourself. Instead of anguishing, "Why can't we all just be happy?" try to detach and watch everyone take on their roles as if you were watching a play. Decide not to be drawn into the role you had as a child. Don't resist your feelings, just observe them without judgment.

Instead of straining for an absolutely wonderful emotionally intense holiday season, and then feeling let down when it doesn't happen, aim for just a pleasant time. Enjoy all the amazing things that happen.

74. aimless

setting goals

Why have goals? Goals give life meaning. It's a human characteristic to strive for meaning and significance. You feel more alive when you have something to aim for—that's why people who go through a war or other national emergency often think back on it as a time when they felt purposeful and motivated.

Reach for something seemingly impossible. Even if you only get halfway there, you're way ahead of where you started.

If you don't know where you are going, you become Play-Doh in the hands of fate and other people.

Make goals measurable: You must have a way of knowing how close you are getting to where you want to be. Decide how you will gauge your progress. You could rate the success of your exercise program by trying to reach a number on the scale, or a specific blood pressure level, or just by how good your body feels.

Make goals specific. Move from "I want to be self-employed one day," to "I want to open a boutique in six months."

Make goals achievable. Break them down into steps. Work out your timeline. Visualize achieving what you want. Instead of thinking, "I wish I had a boyfriend," think "How can I meet good men?" If your dream requires financial sacrifice, try to incorporate this into the goal. See if you can brainstorm a way of getting paid for what you want to do.

"If you want to do something, you find a way. If you don't want to do something, you find an excuse."
—Arab proverb

Make goals realistic. Assess both the inner and outer resources you have to achieve a goal. If you want to learn a language, think about the ways you'll be most motivated to speak it, as well as whether you'll buy tapes or grammar texts.

Make goals time-oriented, because open-ended goals don't work. Build in an end result that you want to achieve. Don't just think "I want to write a novel." Plan to write a certain number of words by a specific date, and work out the steps you'll need to get to that point.

There's a tremendous amount of satisfaction in reaching a goal. Congratulate yourself on meeting even small ones. And don't wait until the whole goal is achieved—delight in fulfilling any part of it.

FRAGMENTED

living in the moment

There are two ways of experiencing life—either way is valid, and we usually move from one to another unconsciously. But if you are aware of the difference, you can choose how you want to perceive things. When you are deeply involved in something—straining to reach the finish line in a marathon, singing your heart out, or leaping into a swimming pool—you are totally involved in the action. Your body reacts, you feel emotionally aroused, and every part of you is totally involved in the experience. This is, of course, the best way to be when you are having a good time. When you are laughing with friends, hugging your kids, or enjoying a meal, you should be completely "inside" what's going on. The other way of experiencing is when you are aware of being in the audience, detached, observing, noticing your reaction, looking at yourself as if on the outside, and emotionally cut off from what's going on. This is a useful way of getting distance from unhappy times. People who have been abused as children often do this automatically, as a way of protecting themselves from pain.

If you feel yourself slipping into an observer mode, bring yourself back by reminding yourself of the reason you are there. For example, at a job interview, you might become aware of your own voice and think, "I'm making a fool of myself." Instead, concentrate on the process, which is simply finding out whether you and the company are a good match.

"Live all you can; it's a mistake not to."
—Henry James

Waiting until the weekend or a night out to enjoy life is like waiting until you retire before you have fun. This moment is all you have. You won't reach anything better.

When you were a child, you were always present-moment oriented. To be in the "now," try to regain that feeling.

Honor the ordinary. Walking the dog, watering the potted plants, doing whatever you are doing with awareness. That is, focus your mind on whatever your muscles and senses are engaged in. If you are doing the dishes, notice the warmth of the water; pay attention to your movements, your breathing, the crockery you touch. Feel the miracle of life, of all your senses functioning, right now.

Most people remember compliments for a few minutes and criticism for years.

Don't try to change your loved ones. Love them just the way they are. It will be a burden lifted from your shoulders— and theirs.

Have you been together with your partner so long that when gift-giving occasions come around, you simply show your loved one a catalogue with a page corner turned down and your choice circled? Do this instead: Exchange your gift lists; then see how you can combine them. You want to learn to tango and he wants to travel? You could both travel to Rio to take dancing lessons.

People who have the most beautiful friendships are people who value friendships very highly.

Respect the feelings of those closest to you. Agree to stop doing one little thing that annoys him if he'll agree to stop doing one little thing that drives you crazy.

When we talk to each other, we unconsciously choose between three modes. Sometimes we use a parent-type voice ("I'm taking you to the doctor!"). Sometimes we use an adult-type voice ("Do you think you should go to the doctor?"), and sometimes we use a child-type voice ("I'm scared!"). If your partner is sick, a parent-type voice is appropriate, but in general, good communication is easiest when you are both in the same mode.

76. Nurturing

giving strokes

Everyone needs to be recognized by others. Shaking hands, saying, "Hi," being told you look good today, being thanked for doing the laundry—these are indications that someone else acknowledges your existence. Eric Berne has termed these interactions "strokes" as part of his transactional analysis theory. Strokes are an essential part of human interaction—we all need strokes to thrive. To nurture the people in your life, give them strokes often. It'll make you both feel happier. Give yourself strokes, too.

Be sure enough of yourself to ask for nurturing when you need it. Ask someone for a back rub or to tell you a joke or give you a hug. He or she will then feel able to ask the same of you. It's healthier to ask for what you need than to seethe inside, thinking, "If he really loved me, he'd know what I need and I wouldn't have to ask."

The art of giving a compliment: Use the word *you*. Instead of saying "I like your dress," say "You always wear the most wonderful colors!" And a compliment that is unconditional ("I like you!") is nicer than one that depends on a particular behavior ("I like you when you smile").

Is it the *having* or the *getting* of possessions that makes you happiest? Collectors get a high from completing a set, tracking down the last piece—when they have a full set, they are in control. Why do you need to acquire so many material possessions? What void are you trying to fill? A continual need to acquire objects is sometimes really a need to fill an emotional void.

If you can't do away with attachments, attach yourself to the good things in life—love, laughter, memories!

If you are not enjoying life with the possessions you have now, having more won't help. We choose to feel fulfilled or not.

Your possessions are tools to help you through life, resources that help you achieve goals: the picture that makes you feel happy whenever you look at it, the suit that helps get you a corner office. Knowing how an object helps you makes it easier to decide what you really need.

Know that when you lust after an object, what you really want are the feelings you associate with it. Discover what your soul hungers for by asking yourself how it will feel when you've acquired the car, the shoes, or whatever it is that seems to be all that is standing between you and happiness. Try to get those feelings (pride? self-worth? satisfaction?) in more meaningful ways.

77. Acquisitive

possessions as tools

The law of things: When you get rid of something old and unnecessary, you open the way for something new and better—it's true of possessions and of outdated, limiting ideas, too.

If you fear losing what you have, that fear will limit your enjoyment of what you have.

When you long to own a specific item, visualize buying it and loving it—but then also visualize yourself getting tired of it and throwing it away. You may find you don't need to buy it.

If you find yourself moving objects from closet to closet—rearranging the deck chairs on the *Titanic*, as it were—objects are creating stress for you. Acquiring and caring for possessions tends to waste a lot of time, obstruct thinking, and replace more satisfying values. The less you need to be happy, the happier you'll be.

"Lives based on having are less free than lives based either on doing or being."

—William James

If you want to connect more with people, start by smiling at strangers, thanking the bus driver, being warmer to those you work with, reconnecting with friendships you've let slide. Start talking to people you know only by sight. In the elevator, for example, compliment someone on a part of his clothing that invites comment, like a message T-shirt. Or remark on a shared experience—the weather, the early hour, your immediate environment—rather than making a personal observation like "I hate this place." Originality is not important, connecting with people is.

> Remind yourself of what you have in common with someone instead of what separates you.

A good conversation isn't an interview.

As soon as possible, move away from the initial question-and-answer format, which forces the other person to do all the work, to dialogue and discussion. Pick up on topic openings your partner offers, and offer openings of your own. Give an answer he can run with. Ask a leading, provocative question to get someone to talk about a subject close to his heart, strike an emotional chord. And when you are with someone, be completely *there*; focus on him totally, value him.

> *"Love is but the discovery of ourselves in others, and the delight in the recognition."*
> —Alexander Smith

78. sociable

gaining rapport

When you meet a friend, be alert to her **"presenting problem."** What is the first thing she talks about, what concern is uppermost in her mind? Offer appreciation and validation. If someone tells you how hard she is working, confirm that her work is appreciated. You don't need to entertain people when you talk to them—let them shine; let them have a turn at being on the receiving end of laughter and applause.

"The only way to have a friend is to be one."
—Ralph Waldo Emerson

Don't pretend to find a person interesting—find out what makes him or her interesting.

Seek people who respect and appreciate you, and respect and appreciate people you choose to be with. Be around happy people—moods are contagious. Let others infect you with their happiness; don't bring them down.

A fear of social situations is often a fear of being judged by others as harshly as you judge yourself. When interacting with someone on a one-to-one basis, we feel we can control how we're perceived. If it's difficult for you to establish rapport with a crowd, try working on your self-esteem.

79. UNmotivated

getting where you want to be

What kind of motivation has helped you reach goals in the past? What arouses your determination? You can use that same motivation again and again.

Write down your wishes and dreams, or they'll stay just wishes and dreams. A written-down goal becomes a commitment. Or create a collage. Do this for concrete goals like getting a new job, but also for making tangible the qualities you want more of in life. Take a large piece of cardboard, paste a picture of yourself in the center, and surround it with images and words from magazines and catalogues that symbolize what you want.

When you choose a goal, all your senses immediately start gathering information about it, you become attuned to anything relating to it and you program yourself.

Build rewards into an action so you'll keep doing it—run with a friend to get companionship as well as exercise; learn to cook by starting with the dishes you love to eat.

Motivate yourself by becoming totally involved in your desire. Bring your goal to life: feel it, smell it, give it texture, picture the ideal end result. Think about the outcome so much that your subconscious feels as if your aim has already been achieved.

There are two kinds of motivation: internal and external. Internal motivation is the inner satisfaction you will derive from the outcome. External motivation is the public acclaim that will make you feel your effort was worthwhile. Which kind of motivation drives you? If outer motivation is the only kind you look for, why aren't you doing anything just for yourself?

Motivation comes from knowing how you'll feel when you get where you want to go. If your goals are not in line with your real desires, you'll still feel frustrated after you've reached them. You decide you need a big house so you can entertain more often, for example—but if the feeling you really want is to be close to people, more space may not be your most immediate need. Keep searching for the real feeling you want—to feel part of a couple, to feel in control of your life, to feel admired— and you'll find your genuine motivation.

Dress the part.
Put on the persona and costume of what you want to be and you are halfway to being it.

If you continually give up before you reach a goal, you are aiming either too high or too low.

80. humiliated

combating self-flagellation

We all talk to ourselves; you may be so used to it that you are not even aware of it. Self-talk is our interpretation of our thoughts. You can't stop thoughts popping into your head, but you can decide not to hold onto them and not to misinterpret them.

> "It is hard to fight an enemy who has outposts in your head."
> —Sally Kempton

Negative self-talk is a bad habit that you should give up for your own emotional health. Why? Because the words you use to talk to yourself create the world you live in. Imagine being followed by someone constantly finding fault with you—you'd hate it. So what gives you the right to do the same thing to yourself? You shouldn't live in a body where you never allow yourself to feel loved. If you can't feel at peace and comfortable with yourself, you can never be truly happy. Become aware of the destructive effect of negative self-talk and you'll make the effort to stop.

When you become aware that your thoughts have turned self-critical, imagine them as a discordant radio station, and turn the volume way down.

Where do harsh inner voices come from? They are remembered scoldings from parents and grade-school teachers, the voices of jealous siblings, and schoolbook maxims, all mixed up and internalized—that is, they've become your conscience. Your mind is trying to protect you from others' criticism today by recreating those voices. Like a well-meaning but deluded friend, it is trying to be first with any negative comments that might be made about your behavior. These voices are learned, which means it's possible to learn how to talk to yourself with a good, positive voice instead.

> *"One of the classic mistakes all addicts make is blaming and hating that part of themselves that drives their addiction."*
>
> —Martha Beck

Humiliating self-talk seems automatic. How do you give it up? The first step is simply to notice it. Be aware of what's really going on in your mind; describe your thoughts to yourself. When someone's late, for example, acknowledge that you're angry, even if what you are saying to yourself sounds like self-blame. As with any bad habit, you must have constant vigilance if you want to stop. You'll need to divert your thinking many times a day until you learn not to respond to your thoughts negatively.

The principles outlined here are based on cognitive behavior therapy and the work of Aaron Beck.

81. POWERFUL

using your mind's eye

Mentally rehearsing what you want to happen prepares your mind and body to make it happen, like placing an order at a restaurant. We all have powerful imaginative abilities that we can use to picture ourselves succeeding and achieving and coping. Sports psychologists know that visualizing how you want to be enhances confidence and primes the neuromuscular system to react in a way that will achieve it.

If you don't like what is happening in your life (the effect), look at what you are doing (the cause). How are you preventing yourself from living the life you want? You have the power to change.

Use visualization not only to bring positive things into your life, but to send negative things farther away. Imagine yourself floating out of reach of past, ugly events. If the memory returns, relive it as an observer rather than as a participant. Detach yourself from the feelings associated with it.

To change the way you want to act, visualize the "old you" projected on a huge movie screen. Now create an image of how you *want* to be and place it in the bottom left corner of the screen. Make this small picture of the "new you" really clear and powerful. Now imagine it zooming up to obliterate the large, negative picture. The good, new you becomes big and colorful; the old you shrivels to a small, black-and-white image. To work, this movie has to be realistic. It must reflect your best self, not you behaving in an unnatural way. You must feel positive about the new behavior and visualize it as specifically as possible.

It's your imagination that constructs the limitations you see, so use imagination to get rid of them.

Want a dream to come true? Imagine yourself achieving it and how you would feel when you knew it had happened. When that picture is clear, "freeze" it, and, keeping it in your mind's eye, lift it up over the timeline of your life; then let it go so it floats down into the right place in your future. Watch it settle on the timeline and see all the events between then and now realign themselves to support the outcome.

If you act like you're a powerful person, then powerful things happen to you.

To find out more about how our minds respond to imagery, investigate neurolinguistic programming (NLP).

82. Apprehensive
fear of change

Do you think you must change for the better before you can really like and accept yourself? It actually works the other way around: When you like and accept yourself, you'll be able to change.

Seek out other people who have made the same sort of changes in their lives as you want to make in yours. Talking with them will help put the negative aspects in perspective. The more information you have, the better prepared you'll be. Well-meaning but clueless friends might reinforce your fear if you talk to them about something that's unknown to them.

If you want to change your behavior but can't, think about whether you are gaining anything from it. Often we stay in a bad situation because there is a hidden benefit to it that we don't want to give up. The only way a hypochondriac might have of getting the sympathy and the concern of friends, for example, is by having symptoms.

> When you make a major life change, realize that you may go through a period of mourning. This can be so painful that we sometimes find it easier to blame someone or something else rather than accept the change.

"Life shrinks or expands in proportion to one's courage."
—Anaïs Nin

Our fear of the unknown served an evolutionary purpose. That fear may no longer be necessary, but it still has to be overcome when we want to reach for what we need.

Work out the overall direction of where you want to go before you make a life change. Visualize the end result. Put your true passion first and everything else will fall into place. The change will be easy if it is in the right direction.

"The best way out is always through."
—Robert Frost

"You can either waltz boldly onto the floor of life . . . or you can sit quietly by the wall and recede in the shadows of fear and self-doubt."
—Oprah Winfrey

When a crisis forces you to change, you may experience panic and a sensation that everything is spinning out of control—this is sometimes called a nervous breakdown. The terrifying feelings come when you are forced to accept a part of yourself that you've denied, and your consciousness is actively resisting. Try letting go and riding out the pain.

Is your fear of change the fear of what other people will think? Channel that energy—of gaining approval—into making changes for *you*.

To set yourself free from perfectionism, learn to welcome serendipity, to be open to the happy chance, to become comfortable with instability and unpredictability.

"We do not need the perfectly designed chair; we want a capacity for relaxation even on a bed of nails."
—Quentin Crisp

Did you have a chaotic childhood? Your obsession with neatness may be the way you're still striving to gain control and get order in your life. Children of alcoholics often have a need to try to eliminate the unpredictable behavior of their childhood. You may feel driven to do the "correct" thing in order to feel safe. Perhaps perfectionism is a way of feeling good about yourself, or of distancing yourself from others. And if your parents were never satisfied with what you achieved, you probably grew up being overconcerned with minor flaws in your accomplishments. Find out what you gain by being a perfectionist, and learn to show yourself the same kindness and courtesy in your thinking that you show strangers out loud.

A cat licking a kitten isn't concerned about whether it's doing a good job. If the kitten feels loved and the cat is happy, then the job was done well, whether the kitten is clean afterward or not. Enjoy the task, not the outcome.

Caring more for order than for people is a mistake.

83. DRIVEN

letting go of perfectionism

People who don't think they'll be respected for who they are sometimes hide themselves behind their work so they'll be respected for what they do.

Is your happiness based on the distance between the way things are and the way they ought to be? When you focus on what's wrong, you ignore what's right. Try to accept the inevitability of life, decay, death, and the fact that anything that can go wrong usually does.

Does what I'm doing really have to be this complicated? Is it really worth doing well? What will happen if it isn't done perfectly? How important will this be five years from now? The problem is not in having high standards or working hard, but in feeling driven, paying more attention to your expectations than to reality. If you try to be all things to all people, *you* disappear.

"By not trying to control the uncontrollable, we get what we thought we'd get if we were in control."

—Martha Beck

The healthy pursuit of excellence is motivated by enthusiasm, not fear.

84. *Scared*

freeing yourself of phobias

Anxiety disorders, panic disorders, and inappropriate, life-disrupting phobias are learned responses, which means they can be unlearned. Behavior-modification techniques can help by teaching you how to stay relaxed. The goal is to give up not only the fear, but also the avoidance mechanisms used for dealing with the fear.

"A life lived in fear is a life half-lived."
—Baz Luhrmann

Phobias can arise when a fear is projected onto a group of people or things. For example, when children can't express their anxiety, they may develop a fear of the dark, or of dogs, or become obsessive-compulsive.

If you get panic attacks, try preparing for them. Decide on a course of action and devise a plan for each stage of the attack. What resources do you have? Can you call someone who will listen calmly? Imagine working through each step of the plan until you feel relaxed. To get a feeling of detachment, visualize yourself leaving your body and walking away from it.

If you see a snake in a movie, you know it can't really hurt you. Instead, it's anxiety that you feel, and as you watch, you realize that the anxiety doesn't hurt. This is the healthy way to deal with fear—exert intellectual control over it. You can consciously push anxiety out of your awareness.

Fear was an important survival mechanism in our evolution, alerting us to potential harm. Some fear is good—it reminds us to drive carefully, to watch over toddlers, and to turn off the stove. Legitimate fear lets you know you are in a risky situation. It's a feeling to act on. Worry is thinking about what might happen and fantasizing the worst, and making yourself fearful by jumping to worst-case conclusions. Try to face a fearful situation head-on and deal with it rather than avoid it.

You have a phobia when you avoid a situation because you don't think you could handle the anxiety. Repeated avoidance will reinforce the fear. The only way you will overcome the phobia is by facing up to it—in time, the anxiety will dissipate.

Everyone is afraid sometimes. In fact, our default reaction is to be afraid of anything new and different. However, we can reason our way through fear intellectually, and understand that we may have to do something that is not really harmful, but makes us anxious.

What happens in therapy? You talk to the therapist about whatever is worrying you. Her relaxed acceptance of all you tell her gives you reassurance that it's safe to face your most painful emotions. A good therapist will reflect back to you an unbiased view of how you appear to other people, and help you clarify the positive and negative aspects of your thinking.

How do you know when you need help? When an issue is intruding on your life, making it difficult to concentrate, and disrupting relationships. It's not so much what kind of complaint you have, but how strongly it affects you.

Counseling is a short-term solution, and its purpose is to resolve specific problems such as bereavement. Psychotherapy is a longer-term situation and deals with deep personal issues, such as a recurring problem with relationships or irrational fears.

The very fact that you want help means that you can be helped.

A therapist doesn't give you the answers, but helps you find them for yourself.

Wouldn't talking to a friend be just as good? Friends are sometimes too close to you to be objective, too polite to be honest, and they aren't trained to lead you through your emotions safely. A friend can be a sympathetic listener and give great advice, but usually hasn't the time or patience for sustained support. And a friend brings wisdom based on things he's found out from coping with his own problems, which may not be valid for you.

85. *Needy*
find a therapist

Therapists don't tell you what to do—they ask questions to help you discover more about your own feelings. Instead of explaining why you feel a certain way, they nudge you into discovering the reason for yourself, so that the insight has a more profound impact.

How do you choose a therapist?

Her technique is not as important as her competence and sensitivity. Find someone you feel comfortable talking openly with, because it's through communication with this person that you'll get help. Look for someone who has experience in the type of problem you have and whose goal is to help you reduce negative symptoms, help you understand why they occurred, and show you ways to deal with them. A good therapist is one who is good for you.

You shouldn't feel shame at considering psychological help—psychotherapy isn't just for the mentally ill. Good therapy is fascinating, like doing a university course in understanding human nature. It is the beginning of a voyage of self-discovery.

Your basic wants and needs are like a child within you. When you are hungry and tired, you'll get crabby and fretful until those basic needs for food and sleep have been met. Love, acceptance, approval, recognition, and admiration are also basic needs. People who don't give themselves these comforting feelings can also feel fretful and unfulfilled.

When you eat healthful food, you're telling yourself that you're important and you deserve to be nurtured.

Shrug off all your cares for a few minutes each day so you remember what life should be like, and so you can get in touch with that feeling of freedom when you need to.

Some people need to be distracted to comfort themselves, while others need to switch to their creative side. Think about doing the absolute opposite of what your daytime job asks of you in your leisure time. If you work at a computer all day, do something that involves getting your hands dirty, like gardening; if your job doesn't challenge your mind, join a book club discussion at night. A person who has a serious job needs to spend time playing, and a person who earns money doing something frivolous might want to have a socially responsible hobby.

Take new photos of the people who mean the most to you and hang them up where you can see them.

86. dissatisfied
comforting yourself

Manage the good times as you do other important things, like paying bills: Actually write down what makes you feel relaxed and satisfied. Keep a folder of things it might be fun to do, and make an appointment with yourself to do them.

Many people comfort themselves with food or drink or activities like shopping, but later feel dissatisfied. Instead, look for a soothing activity that feeds the soul.

There are two ways you can cope: Focus on solving the problem or focus on alleviating the emotion you are feeling about the problem.

Ask yourself: What is the right balance for me between work, rest, and play? Draw a pie chart of your time. The activities that bring you joy and fulfillment are the ones that really matter.

Slow down when things get too overwhelming. Do one thing at a time. Congratulate yourself for finishing one job before you start the next. Take control of at least a part of the day—turn off the phone, set aside an hour to get organized.

Everyone has different levels of coping—what's stressful to you may not be stressful to someone else. Therapists use a list of 100 stressful things to evaluate patients. Death and divorce are at the top of the list, while getting a parking ticket is near the bottom. To put your current anxiety level in perspective, rate it on a scale of one to ten, one being mild irritation and ten being extreme panic. Does the situation deserve the amount of stress you are feeling? If you rate your anxiety as less than ten, you've probably coped with worse than this before.

Listen to your body. Ask how it feels about a choice you've made, a food you've eaten, or a way of life you've undertaken.

Our moods change during the day, and they affect how we perceive problems. We wake up in a low-energy state, become more active during the morning, get tired late in the afternoon, feel more alert after dinner, and get low if we have to stay up very late. At all these different times, we'll have a different take on what's bothering us. You can be optimistic about a problem at 10 A.M. and anxious about the same problem at 2 A.M. the next morning when you can't sleep.

87. Anxious

the mind/body connection

It isn't situations that upset people; it's how people interpret the situations. Think of the way your mind leaps to attention when you hear a noise in the middle of the night—it could be a burglar or it could be the cat knocking over a potted plant. If you think the noise was caused by a burglar, you'll be petrified. If you think it was just the cat, you'll turn over and go back to sleep.

Anxious feelings alone cannot harm you, no matter how painful they are. You are more powerful than your thoughts. Face up to anxiety and find out where it comes from.

Our bodies respond to our thoughts. Imagine biting into an apple, for example, and your mouth will start to water. The apple is only in your mind, but your body responds as if it were real. And the opposite is true, too— if you hold your body in a slouch-free, confident way, you'll feel more confident. To change your emotion, change your body—look up and out, change your posture, exercise, laugh—project the mood you want to be in. You can begin being the person you want to be this minute.

88. contemptuous
transferring blame

Give up judging others. It's a cumbersome burden to carry around and it reflects your self-hate. Blaming people is living in the past.

"When you say the music is abominable, listen to the sound of your own complaint."
—Alan Watts

Weak people need to blame others to give themselves a stronger sense of identity. People with intensely held views are often people who refuse to admit to their undesirable traits; they are clinging to a noble, righteous public persona.

When you find yourself trying to assign blame in a situation, ask yourself whether in this case blame is beside the point. It often is.

Instead of thinking "I'm stupid" or "He's stupid," change the wording to "That was stupid."

Don't assume everything is always someone else's fault. A person in the habit of blaming others will blame others for everything, even her own unhappiness.

● Are you attracted to a partner by traits you wish you had yourself? People who have repressed part of their own personalities often look for those qualities in others—they fall in love with people who can "carry" all the feeling they don't want to feel themselves. But we may come to hate the very things we love about someone. (He's such a wonderful father—but he always chooses the kids over me! I love that she shares her feelings—but I wish she'd stop complaining!) What annoys you about your spouse might be something you need to deal with yourself. Do you have the same traits, or are you afraid of getting them?

> "Everything that irritates us about others can lead to an understanding of ourselves."
> —Carl Jung

● **The people you are most critical of, and react to most strongly, remind you of yourself.**
What you hate most in someone else is the quality you most deny in yourself. What you love in someone else is what you wish for in yourself. If you have a sneaking feeling that your criticism is unjustified, it's probably a lot more about yourself than about anyone else. We take what disgusts us about ourselves and try to destroy it by hating it in someone else. We are all split into a Dr. Jekyll and Mr. Hyde. You can test this yourself: Examine what you complain about in others and apply it to yourself. Critical of the tall, pretty girl in Accounts Receivable who flirts with the UPS guy when she should be working? Perhaps she makes you feel old and ugly and unattractive.

89. Lucky

Unlucky people are tense and anxious and not relaxed enough to notice unexpected opportunities. They think about things rationally; they're not receptive to serendipity. Lucky people listen to their intuition and respect and act on hunches. They usually have an optimistic outlook and try lots of strategies to get a positive outcome, thereby transforming bad luck into good.

> "There are only two ways to live your life. One is as though nothing is a miracle. The other is as though everything is a miracle."
> —Albert Einstein

To be lucky, trust in luck (or coincidence, miracles, serendipity); trust that life is on your side. Have faith that good things can and do happen.

Many people spend their lives thinking about what they fear most, then wonder why it always happens to them. The things we concentrate on come to us because once you have a goal, your subconscious will select things connected with that goal, out of all your experiences, to notice. (The same way that, at holiday time, when you are looking for presents, your mind evaluates anything you see for sale in terms of being a potential gift.) That's why you should always think about good things, in order to draw them to you.

Intuition probably evolved as a survival technique—a person's ability to quickly decode and assess anything new and unknown could mean the difference between life and death. From babyhood on, we look at other people to work out their moods, so it's no wonder we can interpret subtle messages—that someone wants something from us, that someone is about to get angry. We learn to make quick decisions based on initial impressions.

"Life is a gamble at terrible odds—if it was a bet you wouldn't take it."
—Tom Stoppard

Do you have a superstition that holds you back?

"Sometimes you're the windshield, sometimes you're the bug."
—Mark Knopfler

A hunch is probably a message from your unconscious. Your mind is constantly taking in data, combining it with things you already know, and storing it. If you want to get better at reading people and situations, try visualizing them as you ask yourself a question about them. Take a few minutes to "see" the person as clearly as you can in your mind's eye. Notice what impressions come.

If you can't get what you want one way, try another. Keeping the end result you want in mind, brainstorm to come up with a different way of getting there.

When people behave manipulatively, they blame others for their own frustration or unhappiness. You don't have to allow anyone to treat you like that and it's important not to: By allowing something, you reinforce it.

If you are made to feel very guilty when you say no to someone, you need to have a very clear sense of the boundaries around who you are, and what you are not comfortable doing and being. Let people know with a simple, honest, clear, and direct statement just how you feel. A psychologically healthy person will respect those boundaries.

As a baby, you needed parental attention to confirm your existence and worth. **If your parents were unresponsive, you may have learned to manipulate people by getting them to do things in a roundabout way. Now that you are an adult, ask yourself why you can't ask for what you want directly and honestly.**

Telling someone that you are disappointed in them is manipulative behavior. When things don't go the way we expected them to, it means that our interpretation was wrong. A more positive reaction is curiosity. Situations where we feel disappointed can lead to wisdom if we allow ourselves to learn.

"The direct use of force is such a poor solution to any problem, it is generally employed only by small children and large nations."
—David Friedman

90. *manipulated*
sneaky controlling

When you are honest with yourself about your feelings, you can tell if others are being honest. You'll recognize behavior that is designed to manipulate, to "make" someone behave in a certain way without asking her directly. Try, yourself, to communicate without endeavoring to control by saying exactly what you think, asking for exactly what you want, and letting the other person decide how she wants to react.

Manipulators use all sorts of tactics such as sulking, name-calling, threatening, blaming, and making catastrophic predictions to get their way. This is emotional blackmail. Most people respond by arguing, explaining, or apologizing, but it's better not to get involved emotionally. Do not defend or explain. Say, "I'm sorry you're upset," but don't attack. When his tactics don't work, the person doing the manipulation will respond by increasing the behavior. Once he's realized the inappropriateness of what he's doing, ask, "Why is this important to you? What is it you really want from me?" Once you have that answer, you can start to solve the problem.

Introverts are quiet, imaginative, and interested in ideas. Their energy is channeled inward. Extroverts are sociable, outgoing, and interested in people and things. Their energy flows out—to people, events, and things in the external world. Introverts get sustenance from solitude; extroverts get sustenance from other people. Which are you?

Treat yourself as you would want your really good friends to treat you. It's good practice for when they are around and comforting when they aren't.

It's easy to connect when you need to: Take a class—any class. Follow your passions and find yourself in a room full of like-minded people with something in common attempting something new. Learn to cook and invite people to dinner. Start a club or hold meetings—what sort of group would be full of the kind of people you'd like to have as friends?

The nourishing experience of being alone is called solitude. To reach it, one often has to go through loneliness and come out the other side.

Exude an aura of neediness and people will run in the other direction. Get involved in interesting things and people will gather 'round to see what's going on.

Instant way to meet people: Take an adorable puppy for a walk!

91. lonely

introvert or extrovert?

If you believe that couples and families are insurance against feeling lonely, you are deluding yourself. Introverts can feel lonely in a group of people; extroverts can feel connected to strangers.

Alone at holiday time? Exuberance and self-indulgence are good at a time like this. Make yourself feel well cared for. Get in touch with your inner child— why not do it by taking a real child to visit Santa and tour shop windows?

What triggers your feelings of loneliness? Loss of a routine, a person, a thing?

If the idea of being alone scares you, think of what you would like to get from a good relationship and figure out how you can get that for yourself when you are alone.

Do you feel that without another human, your experiences are worthless? That when you are alone, you are no one, that you cease to exist? If you can't be happy by yourself and with who you are, you need to ask yourself why. Get to know your truest self; discover what you like about yourself. It's important to do this before you attempt to be happy with a partner.

Don't sabotage yourself by ruining the good times. Don't tell yourself, "I don't have time for this" when you are enjoying something unexpected. Don't say, "I shouldn't be eating this" as you indulge in a second helping. Learn to have pleasure without guilt. Regret is a terrible waste of energy.

"When you stop blaming others, your education has started; when you stop blaming yourself, your education is complete."
—Epictetus

If there's a specific incident from your past that you can't stop feeling guilty about, it often helps to devise a penance for yourself. If you regret not spending time with your grandmother when she was alive, assign yourself a year of Saturdays volunteering at a home for the elderly.

Guilt is what makes humans generous and altruistic. It's an evolutionary characteristic that makes us stick together, help each other, and stay alive. But if your whole life is ruled by the need to avoid other people's disapproval and you feel that you can never meet others' expectations, guilt has become toxic. Instead of punishing yourself physically and emotionally for your perceived shortcomings, you need to examine why you feel guilty and know that you deserve to be free from guilt.

We feel real guilt when we do something wrong. We feel neurotic guilt when we are trying to stop feeling anxious.

92. guilty

forgiving yourself

Guilty thoughts are a way you punish yourself when your image of yourself does not match who you really are, or when you feel you've violated some internal standard, your self-respect, or your conscience. Our conscience comes from our parents and society, and it is made up of morals and beliefs we've been taught and have incorporated into our perception of ourselves. Guilt feels painful because one part of us is at odds with another part. When you feel guilty, you need to evaluate whether your standards and expectations are realistic. Are they really what you believe in?

Your guilt may be based on faulty perceptions. If a friend gives you an angry look, you may convince yourself you did something to annoy her. Later, you realize her anger had nothing to do with you. Your imagination created a problem that didn't exist.

Don't let trivial things chip away at your happiness. People forget. Is your guilt important in the big scheme of things?

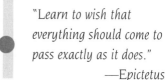

"Learn to wish that everything should come to pass exactly as it does."
—Epictetus

93. bereft
coping with grief

Mourning takes time. There's no shortcut in the grieving process. Sedatives or tranquilizers can slow down healing and lead to depression. Activities that release and express are better than those that suppress emotions.

People show grief physically, by feeling numbness, disorientation, or a tightness in the throat. They feel many conflicting emotions. Sometimes they talk too much, feel crazy, lost, or lethargic, or they sleep too much or too little. They can feel normal one minute, devastated the next. A grieving person often needs to tell and retell his experiences to come to terms with his loss and what he is feeling. These activities are normal and will happen less and less frequently.

Being with the terminally ill: Try to bring your feelings into line with his—it will help him feel less alone. He must leave, but don't leave him first, emotionally. Don't try to control the situation. Let him talk about whatever he wants. Try to subdue your needs; don't make a patient have to comfort you. Let him express anger and fear without engaging in it—look past these reactions to the person you remember.

Nothing can take away the pain, but it is therapeutic to share your feelings. You need to face up to and learn from a loss: Grieving deepens our compassion and understanding. The discomfort of grief forces us to move on, to not cling to the past. Grief creates changes in our thinking that make it possible to cope with the pain.

Shock is the body's way of delaying trauma until it can be absorbed. The bigger the shock, the more detached you feel and the longer the feeling lasts. Hold on to a routine—it can save you. Take care of first things first: Stay healthy, manage the painful feelings, and try to adjust to the situation.

The first stage of grief is shock and a refusal to accept what has happened. Then comes disorganization and despair, which resolves itself into reorganization as you interpret and integrate the crisis and regain former ways of functioning.

If you even think about counseling, get it. A therapist can help you rebuild your view of life.

Millions of people have survived bereavement; you will, too.

94. stalled
overcoming procrastination

When you find yourself resisting doing something, ask: Do I really want to be doing this? What is the real reason I must? If the result of an action isn't important to you, it can be difficult to get started. If it's someone else's project, procrastination may be your way of trying to gain control.

Are you having a problem with planning or a problem with motivating yourself?

Visualize yourself making that phone call, doing the chore. Imagine having already done it; feel the satisfaction.

Are you resisting because if you do well, more will be expected of you? Or to limit your time so that if you do badly, you'll have that as an excuse?

Start first thing in the morning by doing the thing you've been resisting or you'll ruin the whole day by dreading it.

Divide a task into manageable bits—even very tiny little bits—and reward yourself after each.

Be a good coach to yourself: Tell yourself what has to be done in a way that you need to hear. Know when to push, and when to take the afternoon off so you will be more productive tomorrow. The more you try to force yourself, the more entrenched bad habits will become. Know your own attention span for various tasks. Talk to yourself out loud in front of a mirror. Tell yourself what you are *going* to do, not what you *should* be doing. Think of times when you've begun other projects that were just as difficult to get started—what motivated you? Focus on the positive things you can do right now.

Work can be easier to begin when you start with the same ritual every time.

Tap into the fun of the project. Remember the enthusiasm with which you started. Re-create the mood you were in when it first caught hold of your imagination. If you are putting off a project you've been given, find a way to make it fun, and gain control of it by making it more challenging. Devise shortcuts to a routine task, perhaps, or see how quickly you can get it done. Think of the kind of games you enjoy playing: If you like doing jigsaw puzzles, for example, you can get started on a report by matching up similar pieces of information that need to be included. The more something feels like the way you like playing, the more you'll want to play.

95. alienated
your role in your family

For children, even abusive attention from their parents is better than none: They feel that they matter when they are recognized, even if the recognition is painful. The abused child becomes comfortable and accustomed to receiving abuse, and as an adult, continues to prefer that type of recognition simply because he's used to it. He may even set himself up to get it by his own behavior. Similarly, if you felt abandoned as a child, you will seek abandonment by imagining it, or becoming attracted to married or otherwise unavailable people, or even driving others away by your behavior.

> *"Families, like nations, only grow interesting in their decadence."*
> —W. Somerset Maugham

When we were children, our lives depended on pleasing our parents so we'd get what we needed. The ways we found to please them are the ways we interact today with the rest of the world.

Look at photographs of yourself with your family when you were young. What do they say about the family dynamic? Who did you feel alienated from, and why?

Babies need their parents to be a mirror so they can know that they exist. How parents treat a baby is how the baby comes to see itself. Loving parents make the baby feel valued and safe, loved, and lovable—as an adult, he feels worthy of love. Children who didn't get these feelings reflected may still be looking for them when they are grown up, still hoping to get them from others. They spend a lot of time trying to be accepted, and get into relationships that are never what they want them to be. Or they become attached to someone who supplies feelings they can't express, in an unhealthy dynamic such as "nurse and patient" or "rescuer and victim."

We do not see things as they are; we see things as we are.

A relationship crisis—breaking up, divorce—is often a signal that you need to come to terms with your past. Look for patterns in past relationships, think about how you sabotage yourself, learn to give yourself the security and reassurance you are looking for another to provide. Don't blame your parents. Whatever happened in your childhood, you survived it. No one can change what happened to you then, but you make your own choices now. You're in control of your own life.

Out of chaos can come something new and better. Try to find the opportunity that adversity always presents—the chance to improve your life, to emerge reborn, to change your priorities. You have choices. A crisis is a turning point.

Know that, inevitably, moods change. We all have the capacity to overcome setbacks and to recover from their effects, and to feel happiness again.

The way to come to terms with a tragedy is to process and work through your feelings, rather than avoid them. Try to understand how the event violates your expectations about life and shatters your psychological defenses. It is possible to triumph over a crisis mentally, to come out of it more resilient and wiser. The key is to integrate the crisis into your life by looking ahead, rather than looking back.

Midlife crises happen when you start asking not only who you are, but also why you haven't become the person you wanted to be. People deal with this in one of three ways: by ignoring these disturbing thoughts; by giving up their old routines and trying to start over, trying to regain their youth; or by learning to integrate the idea that time is running out into their concept of self (the healthy way).

"There is something liberating about having your worst fears come true—you realize that you have no choice left but to survive."
—Grace Mirabella

Adversity introduces you to yourself.

96. panicky

overcoming adversity

Call someone. Reach out to a good friend to help you absorb the shock of a crisis. And when people extend a hand, take it.

A breakdown is often a first step to greater health: It's the final failure of a lifestyle based on wrong principles. Once the old way of living is seen as hopeless, one can start to build a new life.

Immediately after a crisis, victims often have chaotic thoughts and a huge range of intense, painful emotions, such as guilt, fear, anger, and shame. They may feel unable to cope, unable to continue on. These feelings will ease, but for the first few days it's best to postpone major decisions and put aside destructive thoughts. After a catastrophe, take care of your body, treat yourself gently, and keep to your normal routine as much as possible. Identify immediate priorities—anything nonessential can wait until you are ready to deal with it.

Do you dream of getting even, yet at the same time recognize that this impulse is immature and against what you believe in? Your revenge fantasies are not so much about hurting someone else as restoring what you perceive to be the power balance to what it was before. What you feel robbed of is your dignity and sense of being in control of your life. You want to stop feeling helpless, being a victim, but revenge is not the answer. To achieve closure, you need to take action. You may need to confront someone who has hurt you, or tell someone in authority your story. To feel validated, you must feel that someone has really listened to you and taken you seriously, and been reassured you are not at fault.

Forgiving someone is hard work. Try writing down all your resentment, and continue to write about how you feel every day. Or tell people your story. But each time you retell it, leave out some of your anger. Gradually, the hatred will diminish.

Forgiving someone does not mean becoming a victim. You can forgive but still seek restitution. If you are taking legal steps for justice, you will be more focused if you have forgiven someone enough not to be blinded by anger.

If you must plot revenge, make it a useful exercise. Let your imagination run wild, but instead of acting out, turn your ideas into a bestselling murder mystery.

97. vengeful

letting go of resentment

Duke Ellington, when asked how he felt about being unable to stay at hotels where he performed because he was black, said, "I merely took the energy it takes to pout and wrote some blues."

If you concentrate just on recovering what you've lost, you'll only get back to where you were before. Use this incident to grow.

Forgiveness is a favor you do for yourself more than the person who wronged you. The worst possible outcome would be to nurse a resentment against the whole world for years to come. Why waste time obsessing about it? Why let the person you resent live in your head rent-free?

You feel a whole lot lighter when you drop the burden of judging people or carrying a grudge. When you resent others, you reflect back to the world your own lack of self-acceptance, and stifle your own growth.

Even if you feel you can never forgive, at least let go. Let out the poison.

There are mature ways of dealing with uncomfortable feelings and situations. One is sublimation, which is when one acts out unacceptable impulses in a socially acceptable way (for example, when someone with destructive tendencies becomes a demolitions expert). Altruism and humor are other good defenses.

We tend to cope with frustration the same way out parents did. How effective was that in your case?

Perhaps the most important human need is to feel in control. When we perceive a shift in the power balance, we strive to regain the status quo. Get that sense of power by regaining control of even the small things in life: make a list, tidy your desk, organize your calendar.

Take note of what you are defensive about and ask yourself why. Every negative feeling you have is a chance to learn more about yourself. The more you know yourself, the more secure you'll become, and the less worried about what others think of you, and the less afraid of rejection. As a result, you'll be less defensive.

The opposite of defensiveness is being open to experiences and to your own feelings. It's listening to yourself and trying to understand your own thought processes. It's having an open mind rather than a closed mind.

"There is nothing to hold your negative feelings in place other than your own thinking."
—Richard Carlson

98. Defensive

protecting yourself

According to Freud's psychodynamic theory, we try to protect ourselves from threatening thoughts and emotions with defenses. When what we *want* to do is different from what we know we *ought* to do, the part of our mind that *actually* decides what we do often comes up with an excuse for our actions. Some common defenses are:

Denial: refusing to admit something exists

Displacement: taking out feelings on something other than the real target

Avoidance: staying away from people to avoid our own feelings

Intellectualization: getting caught up in the practical details of a situation rather than face our emotions about it

Projection: attributing our own unacceptable feelings to someone else

Rationalization: making excuses

Repression: burying painful feelings in the subconscious

Paranoia: masking anxiety with distrust and suspicion

Regression: returning to the helplessness of childhood

Don't keep track of whose turn it is. Let go of keeping score. Put the energy you expend in striving to *be* right into striving to *do* right.

Even symbolic threats to our well-being, as when someone our age dies, can make us feel defensive.

"How weary, stale,
flat, and unprofitable
Seem to me all the
uses of this world!"
—Hamlet,
Act I Scene 2

When your painful feel-
ings are numbed by
depression, you don't
deal with them. Until you
can fully feel your own
pain, you won't be able
to let go of it.

Depression is lassitude,
pessimism, and lack of
interest in any activity. It's
feeling drained, emptied,
and hopeless, that there's
no point to anything. When
you feel tired, you feel
temporarily used up; when
you are depressed, you feel
permanently used up.

Remember, depression is treatable.
If your mood goes far deeper than occasional
melancholy, get help. Depression can be
caused by many different things, such as a
hormone imbalance, a genetic predisposition,
or the loss of a person or job. Antidepressant
medication can make a big difference, counseling can ease the pain, and cognitive
therapy can divert the pessimistic and self-
critical thoughts.

**Feeling valued by the people around
you alleviates depression. What can
you do to get a sense of belonging?**

**You may be angry without
realizing it.** Depression often feels like
something that's happening to you, but it is
something you are doing to yourself. It can
be anger that's turned inward. Being
depressed is the mind's way of subduing
pain with numbness. Depression deadens
not only the bad feelings, but all feelings.
It's a refusal to change; it's clinging to
previous expectations.

The first step out of depression is finding hope, a reason to keep going.

99. depressed

chronic melancholy

Plants can't always be in flower, just as humans can't be energized all the time—we'd burn out. And yet, we can't be tired and down all the time, either, or we wouldn't keep ourselves, and the human race, going. We have periods of sadness and periods of happiness—it's how we function. Seek balance by aiming for a middle course and steering by the radar of your moods.

Touch can be very soothing when you are depressed. Find someone to give you a back rub, put on your softest sweater or T-shirt, or take a bath and use your favorite feel-good lotions. Connect with living things. If you don't have a pet at home, go to the nearest pet store and stroke a rabbit, or visit a neighbor's cat.

Try to ease yourself back into the world. Set yourself simple tasks, remember the things that used to bring you joy, get at least a little exercise every day.

100. Benevolent

help for those in the hospital

The ideal hospital visit: Call before your visit, and ask the patient what he'd like: fruit, clothing, reading material? (Don't bring flowers to an asthmatic or chocolate to someone who has just had stomach surgery.) • Knock and ask permission to enter. If he's asleep, wait or leave a note. • Do not sit on the bed unless invited. • If he's up to it, entertain with gossip, jokes, light news, and laughter. • Ask how you can help. Offer to make phone calls or shop for anything he may want. Does the room need straightening? • Let the patient set the emotional tone for the visit. If he says he's afraid, encourage him to talk about it. • Be prepared to leave sooner than expected, and be alert for signs of tiredness.

Don't tell someone who is dying that you dread his death or how much you'll miss him. It's not about you; it's about him.

If you want to spend time with the patient, take photo albums, playing cards, jigsaw puzzles, or crosswords. Give her a manicure, a back massage, or arrange for takeout from a deli, candy store, or restaurant.

"We cannot do great things on this earth. We can only do small things with great love."
—Mother Teresa

Good things to take someone in the hospital: clippings from newspapers and magazines (rather than the whole thing). Notepads, hard candy, lollipops, a child's drawing, cartoons. ● Take things to entertain: a Walkman with cassettes or CDs, electronic games, a kaleidoscope, a windup toy, a light (in both senses) book. ● Take things to make her more comfortable: moist wipes in packets, lip balm, flexible straws, a clip-on book light, a neck pillow, an eye shade, slipper socks with rubber treads, a shawl. ● Or take easy-to-eat food: homemade soup or sorbet in a wide-mouth thermos, lunch box–size snacks, clementines, or seedless grapes. ● Take things to restore personal style: a stuffed animal, framed photos of family, a bed jacket.

Think of ways to give practical help: Research his illness, or drive her to chemo. Take stamped postcards for the patient to send, organize a rental TV or a newspaper delivery or a hairdresser to come to the hospital. Tape a poster to a bare wall, or find a wicker basket with a tall handle for keeping things by the bed. Visit right before the operation to distract him, then restock his refrigerator just before he returns home.

101. Stressed

feeling pressured

Stress is panic that you don't have the ability to cope with a problem. When life is going well, and you are able to cope with everything that comes your way, think about what is making you effective and efficient. Remind yourself of that power and strength on bad days.

Imagine a cat that has just heard a strange noise, or caught sight of potential prey: It immediately becomes poised for action in a watchful crouch, muscles rigid, all senses hyperalert. Humans tense up like this, too; but it's not a good state to be in for long. You know you're seriously under stress when you have behavior symptoms (such as sleep disturbances), toxic thought processes (it's difficult to concentrate; you're easily distracted), or ill health (no appetite, constant headaches). Your body is trying to get your attention.

Reduce outside stimuli as much as possible. An excess of data bombarding your eyes and ears can make it difficult to cope with even normal problems.

Try to eliminate activities that are highly demanding but that you have little control over.

Stress can be as addictive as alcohol or nicotine: the adrenaline rush, the excitement, the sensation of being on a high. If your deadlines are always last-minute nightmares, think about other ways you can get that buzz. The difference between stress and stimulation is being able to choose.

To gain control, identify what kind of pressure you're up against. Eliminate vague, nameless terror by identifying whether your stress comes from paralyzing fears, conflicting priorities, or an overload of tasks. Are you stressed about a deadline? Worried about money? Write down exactly what's bothering you, consider your options, and work out a plan.

There are only two ways to deal with stress: Take away the cause (eliminate recurring irritations, hire a housekeeper, get an extension on the deadline, simplify your routine, delegate tasks) or help your mind survive (learn how to say no to excessive demands without guilt; practice meditation or yoga; take restorative, do-nothing long weekends).

Prepare for stressful periods as much as you can in advance by being organized: Have spares of things you'd be lost without, allow lots of time, eliminate clutter, keep a stock of healthy meals in the freezer.

For stress that is never going to go away, you must be in control of your response to it; it's the only way to survive.